The Big KETO

Air Fryer Cookbook

for Beginners

1200 Days Easy and Mouth-Watering Ketogenic Air Fryer Recipes to Take Care of Your Body and Help You Build a Healthy Lifestyle

Kamren Abshire

Warning-Disclaimer

The purpose of this book is to educate and entertain. The author or publisher does not guarantee that anyone following the techniques, suggestions, tips, ideas, or strategies will become successful. The author and publisher shall have neither liability or responsibility to anyone with respect to any loss or damage caused, or alleged to be caused, directly or indirectly by the information contained in this book.

Table of Contents

Chapter 4 Poultry — 31

Chapter 5 Fish and Seafood — 43

Chapter 6 Vegetables and Sides　　　　　　　52

Chapter 7 Vegetarian Mains　　　　　　　59

Chapter 8 Desserts　　　　　　　63

Appendix 1 Measurement Conversion Chart　　　　　　　66

Appendix 2 Air Fryer Cooking Chart　　　　　　　67

INTRODUCTION

Many people are still struggling with weight loss, if you are one of such people, the keto diet is one that you will love because it has proven over and over again to be a sure way to balance your weight.

Of course, it is good to hit the gym every now and then, but without the right diet plan, you will not quickly see good results. I have been on the keto diet myself and I can tell you that when it is done right, it can be a lot of fun and enjoyable for you.

It doesn't really matter what you aim for, it may not even be weight loss. But as long as you are planning to or are already practicing keto dieting, you should be doing it the right way and with the right cooking appliances — which is why I am introducing you to the keto air fryer.

Though there are many cooking appliances which you can use to make your keto diet meals, you will find out that the keto air fryer will do a better job than the other ones because it is specifically made for your planned diet needs.

Excessive fat is not good for the body no matter the diet plan you are on. It is bad for the heart and can lead to different life-threatening conditions, so the keto air fryer is a necessary cooking appliance to have because of how it reduces fat in your food.

When I meet people who don't use air fryers, I always ask their reasons, and it may surprise you that some of them believe it is not good for special diet plans such as vegetarian and ketogenic — they could not be more wrong!

There is nothing better than being on a diet while still getting the best out of your meals, so an air fryer for keto meals is a development that we should all welcome with open arms.

What you will love most about using this device to cook is the fact that you now have a tool to keep you more committed to your keto diet plan.

Yes, the keto air fryer gives a sense of focus and keeps you maintaining that low carb diet no matter how difficult it gets — you have a higher chance of staying true to your diet when you use the keto air fryer.

Chapter 1 Live a Low Carb Lifestyle With the Keto Air Fryer

Keto is the shortened way of saying ketogenic diet. This is a special diet plan that consists of a very small amount of carbs, proteins, and a high amount of fat.

For you to successfully practice keto diet, all the foods you eat must have high fat, moderate protein, and very very little carb.

Categories of Keto Diet

There are different types of keto diet, namely:

Standard Ketogenic Diet

This is the most common type of keto diet, and it is mostly recommended for people who want to lose weight. To be on the standard keto diet, your meals should be 80% fat, 15% protein, and 5% carbs.

Cyclical Ketogenic Diet

This type of keto is also known as keto cycling because it helps you stick with the diet plan. So if you have been having a hard time staying true to this diet, a cyclical keto diet is best for you.

Targeted Ketogenic Diet

This keto diet is common among athletes because it helps them improve their performance. Even if you are not a professional athlete, you can still practice this diet if you are into serious physical activities.

High Protein Ketogenic Diet

This diet plan is the best for professional body builders because it contains 35 percent protein, 65 percent fat, and 5% carbs.

Ketosis Process

When you are on a ketogenic diet, your body will go through a process known as ketosis in order to achieve the goal you need.

Normally, your body uses the carbs for energy. So, since the keto diet involves a very low amount of carbohydrates, your body will no longer have enough of it to burn for energy that you use every day.

When your body reaches this stage, it starts the ketosis process and burns all that fat you are consuming via your meals to produce things known as ketones.

These ketones are now what your body uses for energy in place of the carbs that are missing in your ketogenic diet.

There are three main stages of ketosis and I will break them down for you.

1. Getting into ketosis

Since your body is used to burning carbs for energy, getting into ketosis is usually the most challenging part of maintaining this diet.

It is normal to feel uncomfortable and hungry, but don't give up because all you need to do to feel better is to drink a lot of water while staying true to your diet.

2. Keto adaptation

After you have entered ketosis, your body will need to adapt to it. Is it not enough to start using fat for energy, you need to keep things going with regular exercise and strategic consumption of carbohydrate foods.

3. Metabolic flexibility

At this stage, you will start enjoying the benefits of being in ketosis and adapting to it. So metabolic flexibility is the part where you start taking advantage of the different sources of energy (fat and glucose) that your body can use in the most optimal way.

Keto Macros: Carbs, Protein, and Fat

As you already know, your keto diet should have very little carbs. So what do you do when you feel hungry?

Yes, you will feel so hungry, especially at that early stage of your diet when you are entering ketosis.

In such situations, what you should do is to eat a lot of fat to satisfy yourself, then drink enough water. No matter what, don't allow your hunger to make you eat more carbs than necessary for the day.

Carbs

With respect to the amount of carbs you should be eating in a day, the main goal is to ensure that you are healthy and getting enough nutrition with what you are eating.

When making your food, you should make sure your carbs are no more than 20 grams in one day. If you can, it is even better if you make it less than that, but for the sake of balance, especially at the early stages, you can leave it at 20 grams of carbs in a day.

As your body enters ketosis, you will not feel any of those symptoms that most people feel — as long as you keep to the right measurement of carbs that you consume.

Protein

As you drastically reduce your carbs, if you take the right amount of protein to work with the fats in your body, you will enjoy so many benefits that a keto diet can offer.

As a rule, you should not overdo the consumption of protein in order to quash hunger. Eat foods that can get you a maximum of 35% calories from protein in a day. That should keep you living and working fine with low carbs.

When you prepare your meals, ensure that you don't eat more than 70 grams of protein in a day — this is a more precise way to eat protein during a keto diet.

Fats

Now, this is the main constituent of your keto diet. You will be eating a lot of fatty foods and this will be your main source of energy.

When you cook, include enough fat to give the meals good flavor. Eggs are a very good source of the kind of fats you will need, beef as well. So get flexible and include them in your food.

75% of the calories that you consume during keto diet will come from the fatty food in your meals.

Foods to Eat Freely and Avoid on Keto Diet

Vegetables

Eat freely	Avoid
Cucumber	Corn
Eggplant	Potatoes
Asparagus	Large amount of onions
Okra	Butternut squash
Broccoli	Beets
Tomatoes	Acorn squash
Celery	Carrot
Mushrooms	Yam

Plant-based Foods

Eat freely	Avoid
Nuts	Dates
Berries	Bananas
Seeds	Raisins
Cocoa powder	Peaches
Shirataki noodles	Grapes
Dark chocolate	Apples
Peppers	Pears
Cauliflower	Fruit juices
Tempeh	Tangerines

Animal Protein

Eat freely	Avoid
Pork	Processed meat
Egg	Breaded meat
Beef	Bacon
Salmon	Plant based proteins
Shrimp	Meat high in nitrates
Mahi mahi	Meat with hidden carbs
Flounder	Lab meat

Dairy Foods

Eat freely	Avoid
Cottage cheese	Condensed milk
Plain yogurt	Animal milk
Cream	Low fat or fat free yogurt
Swiss cheese	Creamed cottage cheese
Cheddar cheese	Oat milk
Gouda	Rice milk

Fats and Oils

Eat freely	Avoid
Butter	Margarine
Ghee	Commercial lad
Olive oil	Peanut oil
Coconut cream	Soybean oil
Avocado	Grapeseed oil
Walnut oil	Vegetable shortening

Beverages

Eat freely	Avoid
Tea	All soda
Sparkling water	Energy drinks
Unsweetened coffee	Tonic water
Black coffee	Kombucha
Lemon water	Sweet wines
Bone broth	Margarita

Foods You Will Eliminate on Keto Diet

For you to always keep yourself in check, a good knowledge of the foods you should be eating is not enough. You also need to know the ones you should avoid and I have stated them in clear details right here for you.

Grains and Starches

Grains and starches are very good sources of carbs. They are used globally for different reasons, including diets that focus on gaining more carbs in the body.

With this knowledge, you can really see why they are not a good fit for keto. Though they have certain important uses in the body, you do not need them in a keto diet, which is why grains and starches can only take up 5% of your entire keto nutritional content.

Starchy Vegetables

Vegetables are good for the body, and they can be good for the keto diet as well, but you have to be careful so that you do not eat starchy vegetables.

Starchy vegetables have carbs and that is what you should be avoiding when you do keto diet.

Most Fruit, Except Small Portions of Berries and Melon

Berries and melons are okay for your keto diet, but if you get too comfortable and eat them all the time, you will not get the expected results from keeping to a keto diet.

As you avoid most fruits out there, use small portions of berries and melon to make up for the gap. Remember, it has to be in small quantities.

Beans, Chickpeas, Lentils, Peas, and Edamame

As you most likely know, there has been a long time argument about the nutritional content of these foods, especially beans. Some say it belongs to the class of protein, while others say it belongs to the class of carbohydrates, but the truth is that beans are actually made of both.

With this knowledge, you can now see why you should avoid them during your time on the keto diet because of the amount of carbs they contain.

Common Mistakes When Following a Keto Diet

Going Overboard With Fat

It is true that we have emphasized the importance of fat in the keto diet, and that is because it should dominate your meals. But one common mistake people make is that they take too much of it.

You must ensure that you do not go overboard with the consumption of fatty foods because instead of benefiting from ketosis, you may start gaining extra body fat, which is counterproductive if your aim of going into the keto diet is to lose weight.

The extra fat will also do more harm than good to your health no matter your current weight, so under no condition should you overdo the fat in keto.

Eating Too Many Nuts and Dairy Products

Nuts are delicious and usually not eaten with cutlery, so it is very easy to lose control and eat a lot more than necessary without even realizing it. So you should be very careful, as too many nuts can cause you to consume excess calories. You could even get cramps and feel abnormally gassy.

Dairy products are also appealing, so as you consume them, ensure you are keeping to the right amount you are meant to have in a day.

When dairy foods get too much, you could easily get kicked out of ketosis and all your hard work will not have any fruits.

Fear of Too Much Protein

Proteinous foods have an important role to play in your keto diet, so no matter what you should not be afraid to eat the right amount you need each day.

If you eat too much protein in your keto diet, it will be hard or even impossible for you to enter ketosis.

So as much as I encourage you to eat enough protein because of the work it has to do for your body, I must emphasize that you should have to follow the rules and never take more than the needed amount of protein per day.

Cooking With an Air Fryer When Following a Keto Diet

How Does the Air Fryer Work?

Unlike deep frying, the air fryer has nothing to do with dipping foods inside hot oil until it gets ready. An air fryer works in a very different way that requires less stress and gives far better results.

In an air fryer, the system of cooking involves a well known method of heat transfer called convection. I will explain this as we go on.

When you finish cleaning and chopping your food, you place them nicely in a perforated basket that usually comes with a new air fryer. Then you insert this basket with the food into the air fryer and turn it on.

At this stage, hot air starts blowing the food and it starts cooking from the outside to the inner parts — this is what convection cooking means.

Is an Air Fryer Good For Keto?

One of the main advantages that make an air fryer stand out when compared with many other cooking appliances is the fact that it is healthier to use.

The food you make with an air fryer is fat healthier than what you bake, grill, or deep fry…and this has become the main reason why people are rushing to buy it, including those that are practicing or are planning to practice keto diet.

Let me list out some reasons why the air fryer is a very good cooking equipment for the success of your keto diet.

♦ I will start by telling you that there is almost no food in your keto pyramid that the air fryer cannot cook. When I say almost, I am referring to foods that don't need cooking before they are consumed — like nuts.

♦ The air fryer is versatile, so you will have fun using it to prepare everything you need for your special keto meals.

♦ If you see any recipe with bread that you want to try, being on a keto diet should not stop you from trying it as long as you use an air fryer.

♦ That seemingly non keto recipe will immediately become keto friendly when you replace the bread crumbs with pork rinds and use your air fryer to cook your delicious meals.

♦ As much as cooking can be fun, no one likes to spend unnecessary time in the kitchen, so it would make you happy to know that the air fryer cooks faster than other methods.

♦ And now to the most important reason why an air fryer is so good for your keto diet — it actively reduces the amount of calories in your food.

♦ With an air fryer, there is little or no oil involved in the cooking process, and while this is not going to reduce carbs in your body, it will cut down the oil you eat and prevent you from consuming excess fats and oil into your body.

Chapter 2 Breakfasts

Spaghetti Squash Fritters

Prep time: 15 minutes | Cook time: 8 minutes | Serves 4

2 cups cooked spaghetti squash
2 tablespoons unsalted butter, softened
1 large egg
¼ cup blanched finely ground

almond flour
2 stalks green onion, sliced
½ teaspoon garlic powder
1 teaspoon dried parsley

1. Remove excess moisture from the squash using a cheesecloth or kitchen towel. 2. Mix all ingredients in a large bowl. Form into four patties. 3. Cut a piece of parchment to fit your air fryer basket. Place each patty on the parchment and place into the air fryer basket. 4. Adjust the temperature to 400ºF (204ºC) and set the timer for 8 minutes. 5. Flip the patties halfway through the cooking time. Serve warm.

Per Serving:
Calories: 146 | fat: 12g | protein: 4g | carbs: 7g | sugars: 3g | fiber: 2g | sodium: 36mg

Gyro Breakfast Patties with Tzatziki

Prep time: 10 minutes | Cook time: 20 minutes per batch | Makes 16 patties

Patties:
2 pounds (907 g) ground lamb or beef
½ cup diced red onions
¼ cup sliced black olives
2 tablespoons tomato sauce
1 teaspoon dried oregano leaves
1 teaspoon Greek seasoning
2 cloves garlic, minced
1 teaspoon fine sea salt
Tzatziki:
1 cup full-fat sour cream
1 small cucumber, chopped

½ teaspoon fine sea salt
½ teaspoon garlic powder, or 1 clove garlic, minced
¼ teaspoon dried dill weed, or 1 teaspoon finely chopped fresh dill
For Garnish/Serving:
½ cup crumbled feta cheese (about 2 ounces / 57 g)
Diced red onions
Sliced black olives
Sliced cucumbers

1. Preheat the air fryer to 350ºF (177ºC). 2. Place the ground lamb, onions, olives, tomato sauce, oregano, Greek seasoning, garlic, and salt in a large bowl. Mix well to combine the ingredients. 3. Using your hands, form the mixture into sixteen 3-inch patties. Place about 5 of the patties in the air fryer and air fry for 20 minutes, flipping halfway through. Remove the patties and place them on a serving platter. Repeat with the remaining patties. 4. While the patties cook, make the tzatziki: Place all the ingredients in a small bowl and stir well. Cover and store in the fridge until ready to serve. Garnish with ground black pepper before serving. 5. Serve the patties with a dollop of tzatziki, a sprinkle of crumbled feta cheese, diced red onions, sliced black olives, and sliced cucumbers. 6. Store leftovers in an airtight container in the refrigerator for up to 5 days or in the freezer for up to a month. Reheat the patties in a preheated 390ºF (199ºC) air fryer for a few minutes, until warmed through.

Per Serving:
Calories: 149 | fat: 10g | protein: 13g | carbs: 2g | net carbs: 2g | fiber: 0g

Cauliflower Avocado Toast

Prep time: 15 minutes | Cook time: 8 minutes | Serves 2

1 (12-ounce / 340-g) steamer bag cauliflower
1 large egg
½ cup shredded Mozzarella cheese

1 ripe medium avocado
½ teaspoon garlic powder
¼ teaspoon ground black pepper

1. Cook cauliflower according to package instructions. Remove from bag and place into cheesecloth or clean towel to remove excess moisture. 2. Place cauliflower into a large bowl and mix in egg and Mozzarella. Cut a piece of parchment to fit your air fryer basket. Separate the cauliflower mixture into two, and place it on the parchment in two mounds. Press out the cauliflower mounds into a ¼-inch-thick rectangle. Place the parchment into the air fryer basket. 3. Adjust the temperature to 400ºF (204ºC) and set the timer for 8 minutes. 4. Flip the cauliflower halfway through the cooking time. 5. When the timer beeps, remove the parchment and allow the cauliflower to cool 5 minutes. 6. Cut open the avocado and remove the pit. Scoop out the inside, place it in a medium bowl, and mash it with garlic powder and pepper. Spread onto the cauliflower. Serve immediately.

Per Serving:
Calories: 321 | fat: 22g | protein: 16g | carbs: 19g | fiber: 10g | sodium: 99mg

Buffalo Chicken Breakfast Muffins

Prep time: 7 minutes | Cook time: 13 to 16 minutes | Serves 10

6 ounces (170 g) shredded cooked chicken

3 ounces (85 g) blue cheese, crumbled

2 tablespoons unsalted butter, melted

⅓ cup Buffalo hot sauce, such

as Frank's RedHot

1 teaspoon minced garlic

6 large eggs

Sea salt and freshly ground black pepper, to taste

Avocado oil spray

1. In a large bowl, stir together the chicken, blue cheese, melted butter, hot sauce, and garlic. 2. In a medium bowl or large liquid measuring cup, beat the eggs. Season with salt and pepper. 3. Spray 10 silicone muffin cups with oil. Divide the chicken mixture among the cups, and pour the egg mixture over top. 4. Place the cups in the air fryer and set to 300°F (149°C). Bake for 13 to 16 minutes, until the muffins are set and cooked through. (Depending on the size of your air fryer, you may need to cook the muffins in batches.)

Per Serving:
Calories: 129 | fat: 9g | protein: 10g | carbs: 1g | net carbs: 1g | fiber: 0g

Mozzarella Bacon Calzones

Prep time: 15 minutes | Cook time: 12 minutes | Serves 4

2 large eggs

1 cup blanched finely ground almond flour

2 cups shredded Mozzarella cheese

2 ounces (57 g) cream cheese, softened and broken into small pieces

4 slices cooked sugar-free bacon, crumbled

1. Beat eggs in a small bowl. Pour into a medium nonstick skillet over medium heat and scramble. Set aside. 2. In a large microwave-safe bowl, mix flour and Mozzarella. Add cream cheese to the bowl. 3. Place bowl in microwave and cook 45 seconds on high to melt cheese, then stir with a fork until a soft dough ball forms. 4. Cut a piece of parchment to fit air fryer basket. Separate dough into two sections and press each out into an 8-inch round. 5. On half of each dough round, place half of the scrambled eggs and crumbled bacon. Fold the other side of the dough over and press to seal the edges. 6. Place calzones on ungreased parchment and into air fryer basket. Adjust the temperature to 350°F (177°C) and set the timer for 12 minutes, turning calzones halfway through cooking. Crust will be golden and firm when done. 7. Let calzones cool on a cooking rack 5 minutes before serving.

Per Serving:
Calories: 398 | fat: 32g | protein: 24g | carbs: 5g | net carbs: 3g | fiber: 2g

Broccoli-Mushroom Frittata

Prep time: 10 minutes | Cook time: 20 minutes | Serves 2

1 tablespoon olive oil

1½ cups broccoli florets, finely chopped

½ cup sliced brown mushrooms

¼ cup finely chopped onion

½ teaspoon salt

¼ teaspoon freshly ground black pepper

6 eggs

¼ cup Parmesan cheese

1. In a nonstick cake pan, combine the olive oil, broccoli, mushrooms, onion, salt, and pepper. Stir until the vegetables are thoroughly coated with oil. Place the cake pan in the air fryer basket and set the air fryer to 400°F (204°C). Air fry for 5 minutes until the vegetables soften. 2. Meanwhile, in a medium bowl, whisk the eggs and Parmesan until thoroughly combined. Pour the egg mixture into the pan and shake gently to distribute the vegetables. Air fry for another 15 minutes until the eggs are set. 3. Remove from the air fryer and let sit for 5 minutes to cool slightly. Use a silicone spatula to gently lift the frittata onto a plate before serving.

Per Serving:
Calories: 329 | fat: 23g | protein: 24g | carbs: 6g | fiber: 0g | sodium: 793mg

Portobello Eggs Benedict

Prep time: 10 minutes | Cook time: 10 to 14 minutes | Serves 2

1 tablespoon olive oil

2 cloves garlic, minced

¼ teaspoon dried thyme

2 portobello mushrooms, stems removed and gills scraped out

2 Roma tomatoes, halved lengthwise

Salt and freshly ground black

pepper, to taste

2 large eggs

2 tablespoons grated Pecorino Romano cheese

1 tablespoon chopped fresh parsley, for garnish

1 teaspoon truffle oil (optional)

1. Preheat the air fryer to 400°F (204°C). 2. In a small bowl, combine the olive oil, garlic, and thyme. Brush the mixture over the mushrooms and tomatoes until thoroughly coated. Season to taste with salt and freshly ground black pepper. 3. Arrange the vegetables, cut side up, in the air fryer basket. Crack an egg into the center of each mushroom and sprinkle with cheese. Air fry for 10 to 14 minutes until the vegetables are tender and the whites are firm. When cool enough to handle, coarsely chop the tomatoes and place on top of the eggs. Scatter parsley on top and drizzle with truffle oil, if desired, just before serving.

Per Serving:
Calories: 189 | fat: 13g | protein: 11g | carbs: 7g | fiber: 2g | sodium: 87mg

Buffalo Egg Cups

Prep time: 10 minutes | Cook time: 15 minutes | Serves 2

4 large eggs
2 ounces (57 g) full-fat cream cheese

2 tablespoons buffalo sauce
½ cup shredded sharp Cheddar cheese

1. Crack eggs into two ramekins. 2. In a small microwave-safe bowl, mix cream cheese, buffalo sauce, and Cheddar. Microwave for 20 seconds and then stir. Place a spoonful into each ramekin on top of the eggs. 3. Place ramekins into the air fryer basket. 4. Adjust the temperature to 320ºF (160ºC) and bake for 15 minutes. 5. Serve warm.

Per Serving:
Calories: 354 | fat: 29g | protein: 21g | carbs: 3g | fiber: 0g | sodium: 343mg

Veggie Frittata

Prep time: 7 minutes | Cook time: 21 to 23 minutes | Serves 2

Avocado oil spray
¼ cup diced red onion
¼ cup diced red bell pepper
¼ cup finely chopped broccoli
4 large eggs

3 ounces (85 g) shredded sharp Cheddar cheese, divided
½ teaspoon dried thyme
Sea salt and freshly ground black pepper, to taste

1. Spray a pan well with oil. Put the onion, pepper, and broccoli in the pan, place the pan in the air fryer, and set to 350ºF (177ºC). Bake for 5 minutes. 2. While the vegetables cook, beat the eggs in a medium bowl. Stir in half of the cheese, and season with the thyme, salt, and pepper. 3. Add the eggs to the pan and top with the remaining cheese. Set the air fryer to 350ºF (177ºC). Bake for 16 to 18 minutes, until cooked through.

Per Serving:
Calories: 326 | fat: 23g | protein: 24g | carbs: 4g | fiber: 1g | sodium: 156mg

Cheddar Eggs

Prep time: 5 minutes | Cook time: 15 minutes | Serves 2

4 large eggs
2 tablespoons unsalted butter, melted

½ cup shredded sharp Cheddar cheese

1. Crack eggs into a round baking dish and whisk. Place dish into the air fryer basket. 2. Adjust the temperature to 400ºF (204ºC) and set the timer for 10 minutes. 3. After 5 minutes, stir the eggs and add the butter and cheese. Let cook 3 more minutes and stir again. 4. Allow eggs to finish cooking an additional 2 minutes or remove if they are to your desired liking. 5. Use a fork to fluff. Serve warm.

Per Serving:
Calories: 328 | fat: 27g | protein: 20g | carbs: 1g | net carbs: 1g | fiber: 0g

Sausage Egg Cup

Prep time: 10 minutes | Cook time: 15 minutes | Serves 6

12 ounces (340 g) ground pork breakfast sausage
6 large eggs
½ teaspoon salt

¼ teaspoon ground black pepper
½ teaspoon crushed red pepper flakes

1. Place sausage in six 4-inch ramekins (about 2 ounces / 57 g per ramekin) greased with cooking oil. Press sausage down to cover bottom and about ½-inch up the sides of ramekins. Crack one egg into each ramekin and sprinkle evenly with salt, black pepper, and red pepper flakes. 2. Place ramekins into air fryer basket. Adjust the temperature to 350ºF (177ºC) and set the timer for 15 minutes. Egg cups will be done when sausage is fully cooked to at least 145ºF (63ºC) and the egg is firm. Serve warm.

Per Serving:
Calories: 268 | fat: 23g | protein: 14g | carbs: 1g | net carbs: 1g | fiber: 0g

Green Eggs and Ham

Prep time: 5 minutes | Cook time: 10 minutes | Serves 2

1 large Hass avocado, halved and pitted
2 thin slices ham
2 large eggs
2 tablespoons chopped green onions, plus more for garnish

½ teaspoon fine sea salt
¼ teaspoon ground black pepper
¼ cup shredded Cheddar cheese (omit for dairy-free)

1. Preheat the air fryer to 400ºF (204ºC). 2. Place a slice of ham into the cavity of each avocado half. Crack an egg on top of the ham, then sprinkle on the green onions, salt, and pepper. 3. Place the avocado halves in the air fryer cut side up and air fry for 10 minutes, or until the egg is cooked to your desired doneness. Top with the cheese (if using) and air fry for 30 seconds more, or until the cheese is melted. Garnish with chopped green onions. 4. Best served fresh. Store extras in an airtight container in the fridge for up to 4 days. Reheat in a preheated 350ºF (177ºC) air fryer for a few minutes, until warmed through.

Per Serving:
Calories: 316 | fat: 25g | protein: 16g | carbs: 10g | sugars: 1g | fiber: 7g | sodium: 660mg

Pumpkin Spice Muffins

Prep time: 10 minutes | Cook time: 15 minutes | Serves 6

1 cup blanched finely ground almond flour	¼ cup pure pumpkin purée
½ cup granular erythritol	½ teaspoon ground cinnamon
½ teaspoon baking powder	¼ teaspoon ground nutmeg
¼ cup unsalted butter, softened	1 teaspoon vanilla extract
	2 large eggs

1. In a large bowl, mix almond flour, erythritol, baking powder, butter, pumpkin purée, cinnamon, nutmeg, and vanilla. 2. Gently stir in eggs. 3. Evenly pour the batter into six silicone muffin cups. Place muffin cups into the air fryer basket, working in batches if necessary. 4. Adjust the temperature to 300ºF (149ºC) and bake for 15 minutes. 5. When completely cooked, a toothpick inserted in center will come out mostly clean. Serve warm.

Per Serving:
Calories: 261 | fat: 19g | protein: 8g | carbs: 16g | sugars: 11g | fiber: 3g | sodium: 34mg

Breakfast Sammies

Prep time: 15 minutes | Cook time: 20 minutes | Serves 5

Biscuits:	Eggs:
6 large egg whites	5 large eggs
2 cups blanched almond flour, plus more if needed	½ teaspoon fine sea salt
1½ teaspoons baking powder	¼ teaspoon ground black pepper
½ teaspoon fine sea salt	5 (1-ounce / 28-g) slices
¼ cup (½ stick) very cold unsalted butter (or lard for dairy-free), cut into ¼-inch pieces	Cheddar cheese (omit for dairy-free)
	10 thin slices ham

1. Spray the air fryer basket with avocado oil. Preheat the air fryer to 350ºF (177ºC). Grease two pie pans or two baking pans that will fit inside your air fryer. 2. Make the biscuits: In a medium-sized bowl, whip the egg whites with a hand mixer until very stiff. Set aside. 3. In a separate medium-sized bowl, stir together the almond flour, baking powder, and salt until well combined. Cut in the butter. Gently fold the flour mixture into the egg whites with a rubber spatula. If the dough is too wet to form into mounds, add a few tablespoons of almond flour until the dough holds together well. 4. Using a large spoon, divide the dough into 5 equal portions and drop them about 1 inch apart on one of the greased pie pans. (If you're using a smaller air fryer, work in batches if necessary.) Place the pan in the air fryer and bake for 11 to 14 minutes, until the biscuits are golden brown. Remove from the air fryer and set aside to cool. 5. Make the eggs: Set the air fryer to 375ºF (191ºC). Crack the eggs into the remaining greased pie pan and sprinkle with the salt and pepper. Place the eggs in the air fryer to bake for 5 minutes, or until they are cooked to your liking. 6. Open the air fryer and top each egg yolk with a slice of cheese (if using). Bake for another minute, or until the cheese is melted. 7. Once the biscuits are cool, slice them in half lengthwise. Place 1 cooked egg topped with cheese and 2 slices of ham in each biscuit. 8. Store leftover biscuits, eggs, and ham in separate airtight containers in the fridge for up to 3 days. Reheat the biscuits and eggs on a baking sheet in a preheated 350ºF (177ºC) air fryer for 5 minutes, or until warmed through.

Per Serving:
Calories: 454 | fat: 35g | protein: 27g | carbs: 8g | net carbs: 4g | fiber: 4g

Cheesy Bell Pepper Eggs

Prep time: 10 minutes | Cook time: 15 minutes | Serves 4

4 medium green bell peppers	chopped
3 ounces (85 g) cooked ham, chopped	8 large eggs
¼ medium onion, peeled and	1 cup mild Cheddar cheese

1. Cut the tops off each bell pepper. Remove the seeds and the white membranes with a small knife. Place ham and onion into each pepper. 2. Crack 2 eggs into each pepper. Top with ¼ cup cheese per pepper. Place into the air fryer basket. 3. Adjust the temperature to 390ºF (199ºC) and air fry for 15 minutes. 4. When fully cooked, peppers will be tender and eggs will be firm. Serve immediately.

Per Serving:
Calories: 314 | fat: 20g | protein: 25g | carbs: 7g | net carbs: 5g | fiber: 2g

Egg White Cups

Prep time: 10 minutes | Cook time: 15 minutes | Serves 4

2 cups 100% liquid egg whites	½ medium Roma tomato, cored and diced
3 tablespoons salted butter, melted	½ cup chopped fresh spinach leaves
¼ teaspoon salt	
¼ teaspoon onion powder	

1. In a large bowl, whisk egg whites with butter, salt, and onion powder. Stir in tomato and spinach, then pour evenly into four ramekins greased with cooking spray. 2. Place ramekins into air fryer basket. Adjust the temperature to 300ºF (149ºC) and bake for 15 minutes. Eggs will be fully cooked and firm in the center when done. Serve warm.

Per Serving:
Calories: 144 | fat: 9g | protein: 14g | carbs: 2g | net carbs: 2g | fiber: 0g

Denver Omelet

Prep time: 5 minutes | Cook time: 8 minutes | Serves 1

2 large eggs
¼ cup unsweetened, unflavored almond milk
¼ teaspoon fine sea salt
⅛ teaspoon ground black pepper
¼ cup diced ham (omit for vegetarian)
¼ cup diced green and red bell

peppers
2 tablespoons diced green onions, plus more for garnish
¼ cup shredded Cheddar cheese (about 1 ounce / 28 g) (omit for dairy-free)
Quartered cherry tomatoes, for serving (optional)

1. Preheat the air fryer to 350ºF (177ºC). Grease a cake pan and set aside. 2. In a small bowl, use a fork to whisk together the eggs, almond milk, salt, and pepper. Add the ham, bell peppers, and green onions. Pour the mixture into the greased pan. Add the cheese on top (if using). 3. Place the pan in the basket of the air fryer. Bake for 8 minutes, or until the eggs are cooked to your liking. 4. Loosen the omelet from the sides of the pan with a spatula and place it on a serving plate. Garnish with green onions and serve with cherry tomatoes, if desired. Best served fresh.

Per Serving:

Calories: 347 | fat: 22g | protein: 28g | carbs: 5g | net carbs: 4g | fiber: 1g

Italian Egg Cups

Prep time: 5 minutes | Cook time: 10 minutes | Serves 4

Olive oil
1 cup marinara sauce
4 eggs
4 tablespoons shredded Mozzarella cheese

4 teaspoons grated Parmesan cheese
Salt and freshly ground black pepper, to taste
Chopped fresh basil, for garnish

1. Lightly spray 4 individual ramekins with olive oil. 2. Pour ¼ cup of marinara sauce into each ramekin. 3. Crack one egg into each ramekin on top of the marinara sauce. 4. Sprinkle 1 tablespoon of Mozzarella and 1 tablespoon of Parmesan on top of each egg. Season with salt and pepper. 5. Cover each ramekin with aluminum foil. Place two of the ramekins in the air fryer basket. 6. Air fry at 350ºF (177ºC) for 5 minutes and remove the aluminum foil. Air fry until the top is lightly browned and the egg white is cooked, another 2 to 4 minutes. If you prefer the yolk to be firmer, cook for 3 to 5 more minutes. 7. Repeat with the remaining two ramekins. Garnish with basil and serve.

Per Serving:

Calories: 123 | fat: 7g | protein: 9g | carbs: 6g | fiber: 1g | sodium: 84mg

Breakfast Calzone

Prep time: 15 minutes | Cook time: 15 minutes | Serves 4

1½ cups shredded Mozzarella cheese
½ cup blanched finely ground almond flour
1 ounce (28 g) full-fat cream cheese

1 large whole egg
4 large eggs, scrambled
½ pound (227 g) cooked breakfast sausage, crumbled
8 tablespoons shredded mild Cheddar cheese

1. In a large microwave-safe bowl, add Mozzarella, almond flour, and cream cheese. Microwave for 1 minute. Stir until the mixture is smooth and forms a ball. Add the egg and stir until dough forms. 2. Place dough between two sheets of parchment and roll out to ¼-inch thickness. Cut the dough into four rectangles. 3. Mix scrambled eggs and cooked sausage together in a large bowl. Divide the mixture evenly among each piece of dough, placing it on the lower half of the rectangle. Sprinkle each with 2 tablespoons Cheddar. 4. Fold over the rectangle to cover the egg and meat mixture. Pinch, roll, or use a wet fork to close the edges completely. 5. Cut a piece of parchment to fit your air fryer basket and place the calzones onto the parchment. Place parchment into the air fryer basket. 6. Adjust the temperature to 380ºF (193ºC) and air fry for 15 minutes. 7. Flip the calzones halfway through the cooking time. When done, calzones should be golden in color. Serve immediately.

Per Serving:

Calories: 533 | fat: 42g | protein: 33g | carbs: 6g | net carbs: 5g | fiber: 1g

Bacon, Cheese, and Avocado Melt

Prep time: 5 minutes | Cook time: 3 to 5 minutes | Serves 2

1 avocado
4 slices cooked bacon, chopped
2 tablespoons salsa

1 tablespoon heavy cream
¼ cup shredded Cheddar cheese

1. Preheat the air fryer to 400ºF (204ºC). 2. Slice the avocado in half lengthwise and remove the stone. To ensure the avocado halves do not roll in the basket, slice a thin piece of skin off the base. 3. In a small bowl, combine the bacon, salsa, and cream. Divide the mixture between the avocado halves and top with the cheese. 4. Place the avocado halves in the air fryer basket and air fry for 3 to 5 minutes until the cheese has melted and begins to brown. Serve warm.

Per Serving:

Calories: 357 | fat: 30g | protein: 14g | carbs: 11g | net carbs: 4g | fiber: 7g

Bunless Breakfast Turkey Burgers

Prep time: 5 minutes | Cook time: 15 minutes | Serves 4

1 pound (454 g) ground turkey breakfast sausage	¼ cup seeded and chopped green bell pepper
½ teaspoon salt	2 tablespoons mayonnaise
¼ teaspoon ground black pepper	1 medium avocado, peeled, pitted, and sliced

1. In a large bowl, mix sausage with salt, black pepper, bell pepper, and mayonnaise. Form meat into four patties. 2. Place patties into ungreased air fryer basket. Adjust the temperature to 370ºF (188ºC) and air fry for 15 minutes, turning patties halfway through cooking. Burgers will be done when dark brown and they have an internal temperature of at least 165ºF (74ºC). 3. Serve burgers topped with avocado slices on four medium plates.

Per Serving:

Calories: 283 | fat: 18g | protein: 23g | carbs: 6g | sugars: 1g | fiber: 4g | sodium: 620mg

Breakfast Cobbler

Prep time: 20 minutes | Cook time: 30 minutes | Serves 4

Filling:	for dairy-free), softened
10 ounces (283 g) bulk pork sausage, crumbled	¾ cup beef or chicken broth
¼ cup minced onions	Biscuits:
2 cloves garlic, minced	3 large egg whites
½ teaspoon fine sea salt	¾ cup blanched almond flour
½ teaspoon ground black pepper	1 teaspoon baking powder
	¼ teaspoon fine sea salt
1 (8-ounce / 227-g) package cream cheese (or Kite Hill brand cream cheese style spread	2½ tablespoons very cold unsalted butter, cut into ¼-inch pieces
	Fresh thyme leaves, for garnish

1. Preheat the air fryer to 400ºF (204ºC). 2. Place the sausage, onions, and garlic in a pie pan. Using your hands, break up the sausage into small pieces and spread it evenly throughout the pie pan. Season with the salt and pepper. Place the pan in the air fryer and bake for 5 minutes. 3. While the sausage cooks, place the cream cheese and broth in a food processor or blender and purée until smooth. 4. Remove the pork from the air fryer and use a fork or metal spatula to crumble it more. Pour the cream cheese mixture into the sausage and stir to combine. Set aside. 5. Make the biscuits: Place the egg whites in a medium-sized mixing bowl or the bowl of a stand mixer and whip with a hand mixer or stand mixer until stiff peaks form. 6. In a separate medium-sized bowl, whisk together the almond flour, baking powder, and salt, then cut in the butter. When you are done, the mixture should still have chunks of butter. Gently fold the flour mixture into the egg whites with a rubber spatula. 7. Use a large spoon or ice cream scoop to scoop the dough into 4 equal-sized biscuits, making sure the butter is evenly distributed.

Place the biscuits on top of the sausage and cook in the air fryer for 5 minutes, then turn the heat down to 325ºF (163ºC) and bake for another 17 to 20 minutes, until the biscuits are golden brown. Serve garnished with fresh thyme leaves. 8. Store leftovers in an airtight container in the refrigerator for up to 3 days. Reheat in a preheated 350ºF (177ºC) air fryer for 5 minutes, or until warmed through.

Per Serving:

Calories: 586 | fat: 53g | protein: 20g | carbs: 8g | net carbs: 6g | fiber: 2g

Cheddar Soufflés

Prep time: 15 minutes | Cook time: 12 minutes | Serves 4

3 large eggs, whites and yolks separated	cheese
	3 ounces (85 g) cream cheese, softened
¼ teaspoon cream of tartar	
½ cup shredded sharp Cheddar	

1. In a large bowl, beat egg whites together with cream of tartar until soft peaks form, about 2 minutes. 2. In a separate medium bowl, beat egg yolks, Cheddar, and cream cheese together until frothy, about 1 minute. Add egg yolk mixture to whites, gently folding until combined. 3. Pour mixture evenly into four ramekins greased with cooking spray. Place ramekins into air fryer basket. Adjust the temperature to 350ºF (177ºC) and bake for 12 minutes. Eggs will be browned on the top and firm in the center when done. Serve warm.

Per Serving:

Calories: 184 | fat: 16g | protein: 9g | carbs: 1g | net carbs: 1g | fiber: 0g

Mexican Breakfast Pepper Rings

Prep time: 5 minutes | Cook time: 10 minutes | Serves 4

Olive oil	4 eggs
1 large red, yellow, or orange bell pepper, cut into four ¾-inch rings	Salt and freshly ground black pepper, to taste
	2 teaspoons salsa

1. Preheat the air fryer to 350ºF (177ºC). Lightly spray a baking pan with olive oil. 2. Place 2 bell pepper rings on the pan. Crack one egg into each bell pepper ring. Season with salt and black pepper. 3. Spoon ½ teaspoon of salsa on top of each egg. 4. Place the pan in the air fryer basket. Air fry until the yolk is slightly runny, 5 to 6 minutes or until the yolk is fully cooked, 8 to 10 minutes. 5. Repeat with the remaining 2 pepper rings. Serve hot.

Per Serving:

Calories: 76 | fat: 4g | protein: 6g | carbs: 3g | fiber: 1g | sodium: 83mg

Bacon Cheese Egg with Avocado

Prep time: 15 minutes | Cook time: 20 minutes | Serves 4

6 large eggs
¼ cup heavy whipping cream
1½ cups chopped cauliflower
1 cup shredded medium
Cheddar cheese
1 medium avocado, peeled and

pitted
8 tablespoons full-fat sour
cream
2 scallions, sliced on the bias
12 slices sugar-free bacon,
cooked and crumbled

1. In a medium bowl, whisk eggs and cream together. Pour into a round baking dish. 2. Add cauliflower and mix, then top with Cheddar. Place dish into the air fryer basket. 3. Adjust the temperature to 320ºF (160ºC) and set the timer for 20 minutes. 4. When completely cooked, eggs will be firm and cheese will be browned. Slice into four pieces. 5. Slice avocado and divide evenly among pieces. Top each piece with 2 tablespoons sour cream, sliced scallions, and crumbled bacon.

Per Serving:

Calories: 506 | fat: 40g | protein: 28g | carbs: 10g | net carbs: 6g | fiber: 4g

Western Frittata

**Prep time: 10 minutes | Cook time: 19 minutes |
Serves 1 to 2**

½ red or green bell pepper, cut
into ½-inch chunks
1 teaspoon olive oil
3 eggs, beaten
¼ cup grated Cheddar cheese
¼ cup diced cooked ham

Salt and freshly ground black
pepper, to taste
1 teaspoon butter
1 teaspoon chopped fresh
parsley

1. Preheat the air fryer to 400ºF (204ºC). 2. Toss the peppers with the olive oil and air fry for 6 minutes, shaking the basket once or twice during the cooking process to redistribute the ingredients. 3. While the vegetables are cooking, beat the eggs well in a bowl, stir in the Cheddar cheese and ham, and season with salt and freshly ground black pepper. Add the air-fried peppers to this bowl when they have finished cooking. 4. Place a cake pan into the air fryer basket with the butter using an aluminum sling to lower the pan into the basket. Air fry for 1 minute at 380ºF (193ºC) to melt the butter. Remove the cake pan and rotate the pan to distribute the butter and grease the pan. Pour the egg mixture into the cake pan and return the pan to the air fryer, using the aluminum sling. 5. Air fry at 380ºF (193ºC) for 12 minutes, or until the frittata has puffed up and is lightly browned. Let the frittata sit in the air fryer for 5 minutes to cool to an edible temperature and set up. Remove the cake pan from the air fryer, sprinkle with parsley and serve immediately.

Per Serving:

Calories: 221 | fat: 16g | protein: 16g | carbs: 3g | net carbs: 2g | fiber: 1g

Bacon, Egg, and Cheese Roll Ups

Prep time: 15 minutes | Cook time: 15 minutes | Serves 4

2 tablespoons unsalted butter
¼ cup chopped onion
½ medium green bell pepper,
seeded and chopped
6 large eggs

12 slices sugar-free bacon
1 cup shredded sharp Cheddar
cheese
½ cup mild salsa, for dipping

1. In a medium skillet over medium heat, melt butter. Add onion and pepper to the skillet and sauté until fragrant and onions are translucent, about 3 minutes. 2. Whisk eggs in a small bowl and pour into skillet. Scramble eggs with onions and peppers until fluffy and fully cooked, about 5 minutes. Remove from heat and set aside. 3. On work surface, place three slices of bacon side by side, overlapping about ¼ inch. Place ¼ cup scrambled eggs in a heap on the side closest to you and sprinkle ¼ cup cheese on top of the eggs. 4. Tightly roll the bacon around the eggs and secure the seam with a toothpick if necessary. Place each roll into the air fryer basket. 5. Adjust the temperature to 350ºF (177ºC) and air fry for 15 minutes. Rotate the rolls halfway through the cooking time. 6. Bacon will be brown and crispy when completely cooked. Serve immediately with salsa for dipping.

Per Serving:

Calories: 626 | fat: 54g | protein: 27g | carbs: 6g | net carbs: 5g | fiber: 1g

Mini Shrimp Frittata

Prep time: 15 minutes | Cook time: 20 minutes | Serves 4

1 teaspoon olive oil, plus more
for spraying
½ small red bell pepper, finely
diced
1 teaspoon minced garlic
1 (4-ounce / 113-g) can of tiny

shrimp, drained
Salt and freshly ground black
pepper, to taste
4 eggs, beaten
4 teaspoons ricotta cheese

1. Spray four ramekins with olive oil. 2. In a medium skillet over medium-low heat, heat 1 teaspoon of olive oil. Add the bell pepper and garlic and sauté until the pepper is soft, about 5 minutes 3. Add the shrimp, season with salt and pepper, and cook until warm, 1 to 2 minutes. Remove from the heat. 4. Add the eggs and stir to combine. 5. Pour one quarter of the mixture into each ramekin. 6. Place 2 ramekins in the air fryer basket and bake at 350ºF (177ºC) for 6 minutes. 7. Remove the air fryer basket from the air fryer and stir the mixture in each ramekin. Top each frittata with 1 teaspoon of ricotta cheese. Return the air fryer basket to the air fryer and cook until eggs are set and the top is lightly browned, 4 to 5 minutes. 8. Repeat with the remaining two ramekins.

Per Serving:

Calories: 114 | fat: 6g | protein: 12g | carbs: 1g | fiber: 0g | sodium: 314mg

Smoky Sausage Patties

Prep time: 30 minutes | Cook time: 9 minutes | Serves 8

1 pound (454 g) ground pork	½ teaspoon fennel seeds
1 tablespoon coconut aminos	½ teaspoon dried thyme
2 teaspoons liquid smoke	½ teaspoon freshly ground
1 teaspoon dried sage	black pepper
1 teaspoon sea salt	¼ teaspoon cayenne pepper

1. In a large bowl, combine the pork, coconut aminos, liquid smoke, sage, salt, fennel seeds, thyme, black pepper, and cayenne pepper. Work the meat with your hands until the seasonings are fully incorporated. 2. Shape the mixture into 8 equal-size patties. Using your thumb, make a dent in the center of each patty. Place the patties on a plate and cover with plastic wrap. Refrigerate the patties for at least 30 minutes. 3. Working in batches if necessary, place the patties in a single layer in the air fryer, being careful not to overcrowd them. 4. Set the air fryer to 400ºF (204ºC) and air fry for 5 minutes. Flip and cook for about 4 minutes more.

Per Serving:
Calories: 70 | fat: 2g | protein: 12g | carbs: 0g | fiber: 0g | sodium: 329mg

Double-Dipped Mini Cinnamon Biscuits

Prep time: 15 minutes | Cook time: 13 minutes | Makes 8 biscuits

2 cups blanched almond flour	1 large egg
½ cup Swerve confectioners'-style sweetener or equivalent amount of liquid or powdered sweetener	1 teaspoon vanilla extract
	3 teaspoons ground cinnamon
	Glaze:
1 teaspoon baking powder	½ cup Swerve confectioners'-style sweetener or equivalent amount of powdered sweetener
½ teaspoon fine sea salt	
¼ cup plus 2 tablespoons (¾ stick) very cold unsalted butter	¼ cup heavy cream or unsweetened, unflavored almond milk
¼ cup unsweetened, unflavored almond milk	

1. Preheat the air fryer to 350ºF (177ºC). Line a pie pan that fits into your air fryer with parchment paper. 2. In a medium-sized bowl, mix together the almond flour, sweetener (if powdered; do not add liquid sweetener), baking powder, and salt. Cut the butter into ½-inch squares, then use a hand mixer to work the butter into the dry ingredients. When you are done, the mixture should still have chunks of butter. 3. In a small bowl, whisk together the almond milk, egg, and vanilla extract (if using liquid sweetener, add it as well) until blended. Using a fork, stir the wet ingredients into the dry ingredients until large clumps form. Add the cinnamon and use your hands to swirl it into the dough. 4. Form the dough into sixteen 1-inch balls and place them on the prepared pan, spacing them about ½ inch apart. (If you're using a smaller air fryer, work in batches if necessary.) Bake in the air fryer until golden, 10 to 13 minutes. Remove from the air fryer and let cool on the pan for at least 5 minutes. 5. While the biscuits bake, make the glaze: Place the powdered sweetener in a small bowl and slowly stir in the heavy cream with a fork. 6. When the biscuits have cooled somewhat, dip the tops into the glaze, allow it to dry a bit, and then dip again for a thick glaze. 7. Serve warm or at room temperature. Store unglazed biscuits in an airtight container in the refrigerator for up to 3 days or in the freezer for up to a month. Reheat in a preheated 350ºF (177ºC) air fryer for 5 minutes, or until warmed through, and dip in the glaze as instructed above.

Per Serving:
Calories: 187 | fat: 17g | protein: 5g | carbs: 8g | net carbs: 5g | fiber: 3g

Vegetable Frittata

Prep time: 10 minutes | Cook time: 19 minutes | Serves 1 to 2

½ red or green bell pepper, cut into ½-inch chunks	3 eggs, beaten
	½ cup grated Cheddar cheese
4 button mushrooms, sliced	Salt and freshly ground black
½ cup diced zucchini	pepper, to taste
½ teaspoon chopped fresh oregano or thyme	1 teaspoon butter
	1 teaspoon chopped fresh
1 teaspoon olive oil	parsley

1. Preheat the air fryer to 400ºF (204ºC). 2. Toss the peppers, mushrooms, zucchini and oregano with the olive oil and air fry for 6 minutes, shaking the basket once or twice during the cooking process to redistribute the ingredients. 3. While the vegetables are cooking, beat the eggs well in a bowl, stir in the Cheddar cheese and season with salt and freshly ground black pepper. Add the air-fried vegetables to this bowl when they have finished cooking. 4. Place a cake pan into the air fryer basket with the butter using an aluminum sling to lower the pan into the basket. Air fry for 1 minute at 380ºF (193ºC) to melt the butter. Remove the cake pan and rotate the pan to distribute the butter and grease the pan. Pour the egg mixture into the cake pan and return the pan to the air fryer, using the aluminum sling. 5. Air fry at 380ºF (193ºC) for 12 minutes, or until the frittata has puffed up and is lightly browned. Let the frittata sit in the air fryer for 5 minutes to cool to an edible temperature and set up. Remove the cake pan from the air fryer, sprinkle with parsley and serve immediately.

Per Serving:
Calories: 297 | fat: 21g | protein: 19g | carbs: 10g | sugars: 6g | fiber: 3g | sodium: 295mg

Bacon-and-Eggs Avocado

Prep time: 5 minutes | Cook time: 17 minutes | Serves 1

1 large egg	Fresh parsley, for serving
1 avocado, halved, peeled, and	(optional)
pitted	Sea salt flakes, for garnish
2 slices bacon	(optional)

1. Spray the air fryer basket with avocado oil. Preheat the air fryer to 320°F (160°C). Fill a small bowl with cool water. 2. Soft-boil the egg: Place the egg in the air fryer basket. Air fry for 6 minutes for a soft yolk or 7 minutes for a cooked yolk. Transfer the egg to the bowl of cool water and let sit for 2 minutes. Peel and set aside. 3. Use a spoon to carve out extra space in the center of the avocado halves until the cavities are big enough to fit the soft-boiled egg. Place the soft-boiled egg in the center of one half of the avocado and replace the other half of the avocado on top, so the avocado appears whole on the outside. 4. Starting at one end of the avocado, wrap the bacon around the avocado to completely cover it. Use toothpicks to hold the bacon in place. 5. Place the bacon-wrapped avocado in the air fryer basket and air fry for 5 minutes. Flip the avocado over and air fry for another 5 minutes, or until the bacon is cooked to your liking. Serve on a bed of fresh parsley, if desired, and sprinkle with salt flakes, if desired. 6. Best served fresh. Store extras in an airtight container in the fridge for up to 4 days. Reheat in a preheated 320°F (160°C) air fryer for 4 minutes, or until heated through.

Per Serving:

Calories: 605 | fat: 54g | protein: 17g | carbs: 18g | sugars: 2g | fiber: 14g | sodium: 329mg

Breakfast Meatballs

Prep time: 10 minutes | Cook time: 15 minutes | Makes 18 meatballs

1 pound (454 g) ground pork	½ cup shredded sharp Cheddar
breakfast sausage	cheese
½ teaspoon salt	1 ounce (28 g) cream cheese,
¼ teaspoon ground black	softened
pepper	1 large egg, whisked

1. Combine all ingredients in a large bowl. Form mixture into eighteen 1-inch meatballs. 2. Place meatballs into ungreased air fryer basket. Adjust the temperature to 400°F (204°C) and air fry for 15 minutes, shaking basket three times during cooking. Meatballs will be browned on the outside and have an internal temperature of at least 145°F (63°C) when completely cooked. Serve warm.

Per Serving:

1 meatball: calories: 106 | fat: 9g | protein: 5g | carbs: 0g | sugars: 0g | fiber: 0g | sodium: 284mg

Spinach and Mushroom Mini Quiche

Prep time: 10 minutes | Cook time: 15 minutes | Serves 4

1 teaspoon olive oil, plus more	4 eggs, beaten
for spraying	½ cup shredded Cheddar cheese
1 cup coarsely chopped	½ cup shredded Mozzarella
mushrooms	cheese
1 cup fresh baby spinach,	¼ teaspoon salt
shredded	¼ teaspoon black pepper

1. Spray 4 silicone baking cups with olive oil and set aside. 2. In a medium sauté pan over medium heat, warm 1 teaspoon of olive oil. Add the mushrooms and sauté until soft, 3 to 4 minutes. 3. Add the spinach and cook until wilted, 1 to 2 minutes. Set aside. 4. In a medium bowl, whisk together the eggs, Cheddar cheese, Mozzarella cheese, salt, and pepper. 5. Gently fold the mushrooms and spinach into the egg mixture. 6. Pour ¼ of the mixture into each silicone baking cup. 7. Place the baking cups into the air fryer basket and air fry at 350°F (177°C) for 5 minutes. Stir the mixture in each ramekin slightly and air fry until the egg has set, an additional 3 to 5 minutes.

Per Serving:

Calories: 156 | fat: 10g | protein: 14g | carbs: 2g | fiber: 1g | sodium: 411mg

Lemon-Blueberry Muffins

Prep time: 5 minutes | Cook time: 20 to 25 minutes | Makes 6 muffins

1¼ cups almond flour	3 tablespoons melted butter
3 tablespoons Swerve	1 tablespoon almond milk
1 teaspoon baking powder	1 tablespoon fresh lemon juice
2 large eggs	½ cup fresh blueberries

1. Preheat the air fryer to 350°F (177°C). Lightly coat 6 silicone muffin cups with vegetable oil. Set aside. 2. In a large mixing bowl, combine the almond flour, Swerve, and baking soda. Set aside. 3. In a separate small bowl, whisk together the eggs, butter, milk, and lemon juice. Add the egg mixture to the flour mixture and stir until just combined. Fold in the blueberries and let the batter sit for 5 minutes. 4. Spoon the muffin batter into the muffin cups, about two-thirds full. Air fry for 20 to 25 minutes, or until a toothpick inserted into the center of a muffin comes out clean. 5. Remove the basket from the air fryer and let the muffins cool for about 5 minutes before transferring them to a wire rack to cool completely.

Per Serving:

Calories: 188 | fat: 15g | protein: 6g | carbs: 7g | net carbs: 5g | fiber: 2g

Bacon and Spinach Egg Muffins

Prep time: 7 minutes | Cook time: 12 to 14 minutes | Serves 6

6 large eggs	(optional)
¼ cup heavy (whipping) cream	¾ cup frozen chopped spinach,
½ teaspoon sea salt	thawed and drained
¼ teaspoon freshly ground	4 strips cooked bacon, crumbled
black pepper	2 ounces (57 g) shredded
¼ teaspoon cayenne pepper	Cheddar cheese

1. In a large bowl (with a spout if you have one), whisk together the eggs, heavy cream, salt, black pepper, and cayenne pepper (if using). 2. Divide the spinach and bacon among 6 silicone muffin cups. Place the muffin cups in your air fryer basket. 3. Divide the egg mixture among the muffin cups. Top with the cheese. 4. Set the air fryer to 300ºF (149ºC). Bake for 12 to 14 minutes, until the eggs are set and cooked through.

Per Serving:
Calories: 168 | fat: 13g | protein: 12g | carbs: 2g | net carbs: 1g | fiber: 1g

Keto Quiche

Prep time: 10 minutes | Cook time: 1 hour | Makes 1 (6-inch) quiche

Crust:	4 ounces (113 g) cream cheese
1¼ cups blanched almond flour	(½ cup)
1¼ cups grated Parmesan or	1 tablespoon unsalted butter,
Gouda cheese	melted
¼ teaspoon fine sea salt	4 large eggs, beaten
1 large egg, beaten	⅓ cup minced leeks or sliced
Filling:	green onions
½ cup chicken or beef broth (or	¾ teaspoon fine sea salt
vegetable broth for vegetarian)	⅛ teaspoon cayenne pepper
1 cup shredded Swiss cheese	Chopped green onions, for
(about 4 ounces / 113 g)	garnish

1. Preheat the air fryer to 325ºF (163ºC). Grease a pie pan. Spray two large pieces of parchment paper with avocado oil and set them on the countertop. 2. Make the crust: In a medium-sized bowl, combine the flour, cheese, and salt and mix well. Add the egg and mix until the dough is well combined and stiff. 3. Place the dough in the center of one of the greased pieces of parchment. Top with the other piece of parchment. Using a rolling pin, roll out the dough into a circle about 1/16 inch thick. 4. Press the pie crust into the prepared pie pan. Place it in the air fryer and bake for 12 minutes, or until it starts to lightly brown. 5. While the crust bakes, make the filling: In a large bowl, combine the broth, Swiss cheese, cream cheese, and butter. Stir in the eggs, leeks, salt, and cayenne pepper. When the crust is ready, pour the mixture into the crust. 6. Place the quiche in the air fryer and bake for 15 minutes. Turn the heat down to 300ºF (149ºC) and bake for an additional 30 minutes, or until

a knife inserted 1 inch from the edge comes out clean. You may have to cover the edges of the crust with foil to prevent burning. 7. Allow the quiche to cool for 10 minutes before garnishing it with chopped green onions and cutting it into wedges. 8. Store leftovers in an airtight container in the refrigerator for up to 4 days or in the freezer for up to a month. Reheat in a preheated 350ºF (177ºC) air fryer for a few minutes, until warmed through.

Per Serving:
Calories: 580 | fat: 43g | protein: 31g | carbs: 20g | net carbs: 15g | fiber: 5g

Spinach and Feta Egg Bake

Prep time: 7 minutes | Cook time: 23 to 25 minutes | Serves 2

Avocado oil spray	Sea salt and freshly ground
⅓ cup diced red onion	black pepper, to taste
1 cup frozen chopped spinach,	¼ teaspoon cayenne pepper
thawed and drained	½ cup crumbled feta cheese
4 large eggs	¼ cup shredded Parmesan
¼ cup heavy (whipping) cream	cheese

1. Spray a deep pan with oil. Put the onion in the pan, and place the pan in the air fryer basket. Set the air fryer to 350ºF (177ºC) and bake for 7 minutes. 2. Sprinkle the spinach over the onion. 3. In a medium bowl, beat the eggs, heavy cream, salt, black pepper, and cayenne. Pour this mixture over the vegetables. 4. Top with the feta and Parmesan cheese. Bake for 16 to 18 minutes, until the eggs are set and lightly brown.

Per Serving:
Calories: 366 | fat: 26g | protein: 25g | carbs: 8g | fiber: 3g | sodium: 520mg

Pizza Eggs

Prep time: 5 minutes | Cook time: 10 minutes | Serves 2

1 cup shredded Mozzarella	¼ teaspoon dried oregano
cheese	¼ teaspoon dried parsley
7 slices pepperoni, chopped	¼ teaspoon garlic powder
1 large egg, whisked	¼ teaspoon salt

1. Place Mozzarella in a single layer on the bottom of an ungreased round nonstick baking dish. Scatter pepperoni over cheese, then pour egg evenly around baking dish. 2. Sprinkle with remaining ingredients and place into air fryer basket. Adjust the temperature to 330ºF (166ºC) and bake for 10 minutes. When cheese is brown and egg is set, dish will be done. 3. Let cool in dish 5 minutes before serving.

Per Serving:
Calories: 240 | fat: 18g | protein: 17g | carbs: 2g | net carbs: 2g | fiber: 0g

Chapter 3 Beef, Pork, and Lamb

Bacon-Wrapped Cheese Pork

Prep time: 10 minutes | Cook time: 20 minutes | Serves 4

4 (1-inch-thick) boneless pork chops	Boursin cheese
2 (5.2-ounce / 147-g) packages	8 slices thin-cut bacon

1. Spray the air fryer basket with avocado oil. Preheat the air fryer to 400°F (204°C). 2. Place one of the chops on a cutting board. With a sharp knife held parallel to the cutting board, make a 1-inch-wide incision on the top edge of the chop. Carefully cut into the chop to form a large pocket, leaving a ½-inch border along the sides and bottom. Repeat with the other 3 chops. 3. Snip the corner of a large resealable plastic bag to form a ¾-inch hole. Place the Boursin cheese in the bag and pipe the cheese into the pockets in the chops, dividing the cheese evenly among them. 4. Wrap 2 slices of bacon around each chop and secure the ends with toothpicks. Place the bacon-wrapped chops in the air fryer basket and cook for 10 minutes, then flip the chops and cook for another 8 to 10 minutes, until the bacon is crisp, the chops are cooked through, and the internal temperature reaches 145°F (63°C). 5. Store leftovers in an airtight container in the refrigerator for up to 3 days. Reheat in a preheated 400°F (204°C) air fryer for 5 minutes, or until warmed through.

Per Serving:
Calories: 617 | fat: 37g | protein: 67g | carbs: 1g | net carbs: 1g | fiber: 0g

Swedish Meatloaf

Prep time: 10 minutes | Cook time: 35 minutes | Serves 8

1½ pounds (680 g) ground beef (85% lean)	Sauce:
¼ pound (113 g) ground pork	½ cup (1 stick) unsalted butter
1 large egg (omit for egg-free)	½ cup shredded Swiss or mild
½ cup minced onions	Cheddar cheese (about 2 ounces / 57 g)
¼ cup tomato sauce	2 ounces (57 g) cream cheese (¼
2 tablespoons dry mustard	cup), softened
2 cloves garlic, minced	⅓ cup beef broth
2 teaspoons fine sea salt	⅛ teaspoon ground nutmeg
1 teaspoon ground black pepper, plus more for garnish	Halved cherry tomatoes, for serving (optional)

1. Preheat the air fryer to 390°F (199°C). 2. In a large bowl, combine the ground beef, ground pork, egg, onions, tomato sauce, dry mustard, garlic, salt, and pepper. Using your hands, mix until well combined. 3. Place the meatloaf mixture in a loaf pan and place it in the air fryer. Bake for 35 minutes, or until cooked through and the internal temperature reaches 145°F (63°C). Check the meatloaf after 25 minutes; if it's getting too brown on the top, cover it loosely with foil to prevent burning. 4. While the meatloaf cooks, make the sauce: Heat the butter in a saucepan over medium-high heat until it sizzles and brown flecks appear, stirring constantly to keep the butter from burning. Turn the heat down to low and whisk in the Swiss cheese, cream cheese, broth, and nutmeg. Simmer for at least 10 minutes. The longer it simmers, the more the flavors open up. 5. When the meatloaf is done, transfer it to a serving tray and pour the sauce over it. Garnish with ground black pepper and serve with cherry tomatoes, if desired. Allow the meatloaf to rest for 10 minutes before slicing so it doesn't crumble apart. 6. Store leftovers in an airtight container in the fridge for 3 days or in the freezer for up to a month. Reheat in a preheated 350°F (177°C) air fryer for 4 minutes, or until heated through.

Per Serving:
Calories: 362 | fat: 29g | protein: 22g | carbs: 2g | net carbs: 1g | fiber: 1g

Pigs in a Blanket

Prep time: 10 minutes | Cook time: 7 minutes | Serves 2

½ cup shredded Mozzarella cheese	cheese
2 tablespoons blanched finely ground almond flour	2 (2-ounce / 57-g) beef smoked sausages
1 ounce (28 g) full-fat cream	½ teaspoon sesame seeds

1. Place Mozzarella, almond flour, and cream cheese in a large microwave-safe bowl. Microwave for 45 seconds and stir until smooth. Roll dough into a ball and cut in half. 2. Press each half out into a 4 × 5-inch rectangle. Roll one sausage up in each dough half and press seams closed. Sprinkle the top with sesame seeds. 3. Place each wrapped sausage into the air fryer basket. 4. Adjust the temperature to 400°F (204°C) and air fry for 7 minutes. 5. The outside will be golden when completely cooked. Serve immediately.

Per Serving:
Calories: 344 | fat: 30g | protein: 15g | carbs: 4g | net carbs: 3g | fiber: 1g

Spaghetti Zoodles and Meatballs

Prep time: 30 minutes | Cook time: 11 to 13 minutes
| Serves 6

1 pound (454 g) ground beef	Freshly ground black pepper, to
1½ teaspoons sea salt, plus	taste
more for seasoning	Avocado oil spray
1 large egg, beaten	Keto-friendly marinara sauce,
1 teaspoon gelatin	for serving
¾ cup Parmesan cheese	6 ounces (170 g) zucchini
2 teaspoons minced garlic	noodles, made using a spiralizer
1 teaspoon Italian seasoning	or store-bought

1. Place the ground beef in a large bowl, and season with the salt. 2. Place the egg in a separate bowl and sprinkle with the gelatin. Allow to sit for 5 minutes. 3. Stir the gelatin mixture, then pour it over the ground beef. Add the Parmesan, garlic, and Italian seasoning. Season with salt and pepper. 4. Form the mixture into 1½-inch meatballs and place them on a plate; cover with plastic wrap and refrigerate for at least 1 hour or overnight. 5. Spray the meatballs with oil. Set the air fryer to 400ºF (204ºC) and arrange the meatballs in a single layer in the air fryer basket. Air fry for 4 minutes. Flip the meatballs and spray them with more oil. Air fry for 4 minutes more, until an instant-read thermometer reads 160ºF (71ºC). Transfer the meatballs to a plate and allow them to rest. 6. While the meatballs are resting, heat the marinara in a saucepan on the stove over medium heat. 7. Place the zucchini noodles in the air fryer, and cook at 400ºF (204ºC) for 3 to 5 minutes. 8. To serve, place the zucchini noodles in serving bowls. Top with meatballs and warm marinara.

Per Serving:
Calories: 176 | fat: 8g | protein: 23g | carbs: 2g | fiber: 0g | sodium: 689mg

Italian Sausages with Peppers and Onions

Prep time: 5 minutes | Cook time: 28 minutes | Serves 3

1 medium onion, thinly sliced	coconut oil
1 yellow or orange bell pepper,	1 teaspoon fine sea salt
thinly sliced	6 Italian sausages
1 red bell pepper, thinly sliced	Dijon mustard, for serving
¼ cup avocado oil or melted	(optional)

1. Preheat the air fryer to 400ºF (204ºC). 2. Place the onion and peppers in a large bowl. Drizzle with the oil and toss well to coat the veggies. Season with the salt. 3. Place the onion and peppers in a pie pan and cook in the air fryer for 8 minutes, stirring halfway through. Remove from the air fryer and set aside. 4. Spray the air fryer basket with avocado oil. Place the sausages in the air fryer basket and air fry for 20 minutes, or until crispy and golden brown. During the last minute or two of cooking, add the onion and peppers to the basket with the sausages to warm them through. 5. Place the onion and peppers on a serving platter and arrange the sausages on top. Serve Dijon mustard on the side, if desired. 6. Store leftovers in an airtight container in the fridge for up to 7 days or in the freezer for up to a month. Reheat in a preheated 390ºF (199ºC) air fryer for 3 minutes, or until heated through.

Per Serving:
calorie: 455 | fat: 33g | protein: 29g | carbs: 13g | sugars: 3g | fiber: 2g | sodium: 392mg

Spice-Rubbed Pork Loin

Prep time: 5 minutes | Cook time: 20 minutes | Serves 6

1 teaspoon paprika	1 (1½-pound / 680-g) boneless
½ teaspoon ground cumin	pork loin
½ teaspoon chili powder	½ teaspoon salt
½ teaspoon garlic powder	¼ teaspoon ground black
2 tablespoons coconut oil	pepper

1. In a small bowl, mix paprika, cumin, chili powder, and garlic powder. 2. Drizzle coconut oil over pork. Sprinkle pork loin with salt and pepper, then rub spice mixture evenly on all sides. 3. Place pork loin into ungreased air fryer basket. Adjust the temperature to 400ºF (204ºC) and air fry for 20 minutes, turning pork halfway through cooking. Pork loin will be browned and have an internal temperature of at least 145ºF (63ºC) when done. Serve warm.

Per Serving:
Calories: 192 | fat: 9g | protein: 26g | carbs: 1g | fiber: 0g | sodium: 257mg

Pork Meatballs

Prep time: 10 minutes | Cook time: 12 minutes |
Makes 18 meatballs

1 pound (454 g) ground pork	¼ teaspoon crushed red pepper
1 large egg, whisked	flakes
½ teaspoon garlic powder	1 medium scallion, trimmed
½ teaspoon salt	and sliced
½ teaspoon ground ginger	

1. Combine all ingredients in a large bowl. Spoon out 2 tablespoons mixture and roll into a ball. Repeat to form eighteen meatballs total. 2. Place meatballs into ungreased air fryer basket. Adjust the temperature to 400ºF (204ºC) and air fry for 12 minutes, shaking the basket three times throughout cooking. Meatballs will be browned and have an internal temperature of at least 145ºF (63ºC) when done. Serve warm.

Per Serving:
1 meatball: calories: 35 | fat: 1g | protein: 6g | carbs: 0g | fiber: 0g | sodium: 86mg

Garlic-Marinated Flank Steak

Prep time: 30 minutes | Cook time: 8 to 10 minutes | Serves 6

½ cup avocado oil	1½ teaspoons sea salt
¼ cup coconut aminos	1 teaspoon freshly ground black
1 shallot, minced	pepper
1 tablespoon minced garlic	¼ teaspoon red pepper flakes
2 tablespoons chopped fresh	2 pounds (907 g) flank steak
oregano, or 2 teaspoons dried	

1. In a blender, combine the avocado oil, coconut aminos, shallot, garlic, oregano, salt, black pepper, and red pepper flakes. Process until smooth. 2. Place the steak in a zip-top plastic bag or shallow dish with the marinade. Seal the bag or cover the dish and marinate in the refrigerator for at least 2 hours or overnight. 3. Remove the steak from the bag and discard the marinade. 4. Set the air fryer to 400ºF (204ºC). Place the steak in the air fryer basket (if needed, cut into sections and work in batches). Air fry for 4 to 6 minutes, flip the steak, and cook for another 4 minutes or until the internal temperature reaches 120ºF (49ºC) in the thickest part for medium-rare (or as desired).

Per Serving:
Calories: 373 | fat: 26g | protein: 33g | carbs: 1g | fiber: 0g | sodium: 672mg

Herb-Crusted Lamb Chops

Prep time: 10 minutes | Cook time: 5 minutes | Serves 2

1 large egg	leaves
2 cloves garlic, minced	½ teaspoon ground black
¼ cup pork dust	pepper
¼ cup powdered Parmesan	4 (1-inch-thick) lamb chops
cheese	For Garnish/Serving (Optional):
1 tablespoon chopped fresh	Sprigs of fresh oregano
oregano leaves	Sprigs of fresh rosemary
1 tablespoon chopped fresh	Sprigs of fresh thyme
rosemary leaves	Lavender flowers
1 teaspoon chopped fresh thyme	Lemon slices

1. Spray the air fryer basket with avocado oil. Preheat the air fryer to 400ºF (204ºC). 2. Beat the egg in a shallow bowl, add the garlic, and stir well to combine. In another shallow bowl, mix together the pork dust, Parmesan, herbs, and pepper. 3. One at a time, dip the lamb chops into the egg mixture, shake off the excess egg, and then dredge them in the Parmesan mixture. Use your hands to coat the chops well in the Parmesan mixture and form a nice crust on all sides; if necessary, dip the chops again in both the egg and the Parmesan mixture. 4. Place the lamb chops in the air fryer basket, leaving space between them, and air fry for 5 minutes, or until the internal temperature reaches 145ºF (63ºC) for medium doneness.

Allow to rest for 10 minutes before serving. 5. Garnish with sprigs of oregano, rosemary, and thyme, and lavender flowers, if desired. Serve with lemon slices, if desired. 6. Best served fresh. Store leftovers in an airtight container in the fridge for up to 4 days. Serve chilled over a salad, or reheat in a 350ºF (177ºC) air fryer for 3 minutes, or until heated through.

Per Serving:
Calories: 510 | fat: 42g | protein: 30g | carbs: 3g | fiber: 1g | sodium: 380mg

Mustard Herb Pork Tenderloin

Prep time: 5 minutes | Cook time: 20 minutes | Serves 6

¼ cup mayonnaise	tenderloin
2 tablespoons Dijon mustard	½ teaspoon salt
½ teaspoon dried thyme	¼ teaspoon ground black
¼ teaspoon dried rosemary	pepper
1 (1-pound / 454-g) pork	

1. In a small bowl, mix mayonnaise, mustard, thyme, and rosemary. Brush tenderloin with mixture on all sides, then sprinkle with salt and pepper on all sides. 2. Place tenderloin into ungreased air fryer basket. Adjust the temperature to 400ºF (204ºC) and air fry for 20 minutes, turning tenderloin halfway through cooking. Tenderloin will be golden and have an internal temperature of at least 145ºF (63ºC) when done. Serve warm.

Per Serving:
calorie: 118 | fat: 5g | protein: 17g | carbs: 1g | sugars: 0g | fiber: 0g | sodium: 368mg

Beef Burger

Prep time: 20 minutes | Cook time: 12 minutes | Serves 4

1¼ pounds (567 g) lean ground	½ teaspoon cumin powder
beef	¼ cup scallions, minced
1 tablespoon coconut aminos	⅓ teaspoon sea salt flakes
1 teaspoon Dijon mustard	⅓ teaspoon freshly cracked
A few dashes of liquid smoke	mixed peppercorns
1 teaspoon shallot powder	1 teaspoon celery seeds
1 clove garlic, minced	1 teaspoon parsley flakes

1. Mix all of the above ingredients in a bowl; knead until everything is well incorporated. 2. Shape the mixture into four patties. Next, make a shallow dip in the center of each patty to prevent them puffing up during air frying. 3. Spritz the patties on all sides using nonstick cooking spray. Cook approximately 12 minutes at 360ºF (182ºC). 4. Check for doneness, an instant-read thermometer should read 160ºF (71ºC). Bon appétit!

Per Serving:
Calories: 193 | fat: 7g | protein: 31g | carbs: 1g | fiber: 0g | sodium: 304mg

Cheese Wine Pork Cutlets

Prep time: 30 minutes | Cook time: 15 minutes | Serves 2

1 cup water	½ teaspoon porcini powder
1 cup red wine	Sea salt and ground black
1 tablespoon sea salt	pepper, to taste
2 pork cutlets	1 egg
¼ cup almond meal	¼ cup yogurt
¼ cup flaxseed meal	1 teaspoon brown mustard
½ teaspoon baking powder	⅓ cup Parmesan cheese, grated
1 teaspoon shallot powder	

1. In a large ceramic dish, combine the water, wine and salt. Add the pork cutlets and put for 1 hour in the refrigerator. 2. In a shallow bowl, mix the almond meal, flaxseed meal, baking powder, shallot powder, porcini powder, salt, and ground pepper. In another bowl, whisk the eggs with yogurt and mustard. 3. In a third bowl, place the grated Parmesan cheese. 4. Dip the pork cutlets in the seasoned flour mixture and toss evenly; then, in the egg mixture. Finally, roll them over the grated Parmesan cheese. 5. Spritz the bottom of the air fryer basket with cooking oil. Add the breaded pork cutlets and cook at 395°F (202°C) and for 10 minutes. 6. Flip and cook for 5 minutes more on the other side. Serve warm.

Per Serving:
Calories: 541 | fat: 32g | protein: 53g | carbs: 9g | net carbs: 6g | fiber: 3g

Chicken Fried Steak with Cream Gravy

Prep time: 5 minutes | Cook time: 10 minutes | Serves 4

4 small thin cube steaks (about	Cream Gravy:
1 pound / 454 g)	½ cup heavy cream
½ teaspoon salt	2 ounces (57 g) cream cheese
½ teaspoon freshly ground	¼ cup bacon grease
black pepper	2 to 3 tablespoons water
¼ teaspoon garlic powder	2 to 3 dashes Worcestershire
1 egg, lightly beaten	sauce
1 cup crushed pork rinds (about	Salt and freshly ground black
3 ounces / 85 g)	pepper, to taste

1. Preheat the air fryer to 400°F (204°C). 2. Working one at a time, place the steak between two sheets of parchment paper and use a meat mallet to pound to an even thickness. 3. In a small bowl, combine the salt, pepper, and garlic power. Season both sides of each steak with the mixture. 4. Place the egg in a small shallow dish and the pork rinds in another small shallow dish. Dip each steak first in the egg wash, followed by the pork rinds, pressing lightly to form an even coating. Working in batches if necessary, arrange the steaks in a single layer in the air fryer basket. Air fry for 10 minutes until crispy and cooked through. 5. To make the cream gravy: In a heavy-bottomed pot, warm the cream, cream cheese, and bacon grease over medium heat, whisking until smooth. Lower the heat

if the mixture begins to boil. Continue whisking as you slowly add the water, 1 tablespoon at a time, until the sauce reaches the desired consistency. Season with the Worcestershire sauce and salt and pepper to taste. Serve over the chicken fried steaks.

Per Serving:
Calories: 527 | fat: 46g | protein: 28g | carbs: 1g | net carbs: 1g | fiber: 0g

Parmesan Herb Filet Mignon

Prep time: 20 minutes | Cook time: 13 minutes | Serves 4

1 pound (454 g) filet mignon	1 teaspoon dried rosemary
Sea salt and ground black	1 teaspoon dried thyme
pepper, to taste	1 tablespoon sesame oil
½ teaspoon cayenne pepper	1 small-sized egg, well-whisked
1 teaspoon dried basil	½ cup Parmesan cheese, grated

1. Season the filet mignon with salt, black pepper, cayenne pepper, basil, rosemary, and thyme. Brush with sesame oil. 2. Put the egg in a shallow plate. Now, place the Parmesan cheese in another plate. 3. Coat the filet mignon with the egg; then lay it into the Parmesan cheese. Set the air fryer to 360°F (182°C). 4. Cook for 10 to 13 minutes or until golden. Serve with mixed salad leaves and enjoy!

Per Serving:
Calories: 252 | fat: 13g | protein: 32g | carbs: 1g | fiber: 0g | sodium: 96mg

Kheema Meatloaf

Prep time: 10 minutes | Cook time: 15 minutes | Serves 4

1 pound (454 g) 85% lean	1 tablespoon minced garlic
ground beef	2 teaspoons garam masala
2 large eggs, lightly beaten	1 teaspoon kosher salt
1 cup diced yellow onion	1 teaspoon ground turmeric
¼ cup chopped fresh cilantro	1 teaspoon cayenne pepper
1 tablespoon minced fresh	½ teaspoon ground cinnamon
ginger	⅛ teaspoon ground cardamom

1. In a large bowl, gently mix the ground beef, eggs, onion, cilantro, ginger, garlic, garam masala, salt, turmeric, cayenne, cinnamon, and cardamom until thoroughly combined. 2. Place the seasoned meat in a baking pan. Place the pan in the air fryer basket. Set the air fryer to 350°F (177°C) for 15 minutes. Use a meat thermometer to ensure the meat loaf has reached an internal temperature of 160°F / 71°C (medium). 3. Drain the fat and liquid from the pan and let stand for 5 minutes before slicing. 4. Slice and serve hot.

Per Serving:
Calories: 205 | fat: 8g | protein: 28g | carbs: 5g | fiber: 1g | sodium: 696mg

Parmesan-Crusted Steak

Prep time: 30 minutes | Cook time: 12 minutes | Serves 6

½ cup (1 stick) unsalted butter, at room temperature
1 cup finely grated Parmesan cheese
¼ cup finely ground blanched

almond flour
1½ pounds (680 g) New York strip steak
Sea salt and freshly ground black pepper, to taste

1. Place the butter, Parmesan cheese, and almond flour in a food processor. Process until smooth. Transfer to a sheet of parchment paper and form into a log. Wrap tightly in plastic wrap. Freeze for 45 minutes or refrigerate for at least 4 hours. 2. While the butter is chilling, season the steak liberally with salt and pepper. Let the steak rest at room temperature for about 45 minutes. 3. Place the grill pan or basket in your air fryer, set it to 400°F (204°C), and let it preheat for 5 minutes. 4. Working in batches, if necessary, place the steak on the grill pan and air fry for 4 minutes. Flip and cook for 3 minutes more, until the steak is brown on both sides. 5. Remove the steak from the air fryer and arrange an equal amount of the Parmesan butter on top of each steak. Return the steak to the air fryer and continue cooking for another 5 minutes, until an instant-read thermometer reads 120°F (49°C) for medium-rare and the crust is golden brown (or to your desired doneness). 6. Transfer the cooked steak to a plate; let rest for 10 minutes before serving.

Per Serving:
Calories: 319 | fat: 20g | protein: 32g | carbs: 3g | net carbs: 2g | fiber: 1g

Bacon-Wrapped Vegetable Kebabs

Prep time: 10 minutes | Cook time: 10 to 12 minutes | Serves 4

4 ounces (113 g) mushrooms, sliced
1 small zucchini, sliced
12 grape tomatoes
4 ounces (113 g) sliced bacon,

halved
Avocado oil spray
Sea salt and freshly ground black pepper, to taste

1. Stack 3 mushroom slices, 1 zucchini slice, and 1 grape tomato. Wrap a bacon strip around the vegetables and thread them onto a skewer. Repeat with the remaining vegetables and bacon. Spray with oil and sprinkle with salt and pepper. 2. Set the air fryer to 400°F (204°C). Place the skewers in the air fryer basket in a single layer, working in batches if necessary, and air fry for 5 minutes. Flip the skewers and cook for 5 to 7 minutes more, until the bacon is crispy and the vegetables are tender. 3. Serve warm.

Per Serving:
calorie: 140 | fat: 11g | protein: 5g | carbs: 5g | sugars: 4g | fiber: 1g | sodium: 139mg

Poblano Pepper Cheeseburgers

Prep time: 5 minutes | Cook time: 30 minutes | Serves 4

2 poblano chile peppers
1½ pounds (680 g) 85% lean ground beef
1 clove garlic, minced
1 teaspoon salt

½ teaspoon freshly ground black pepper
4 slices Cheddar cheese (about 3 ounces / 85 g)
4 large lettuce leaves

1. Preheat the air fryer to 400°F (204°C). 2. Arrange the poblano peppers in the basket of the air fryer. Pausing halfway through the cooking time to turn the peppers, air fry for 20 minutes, or until they are softened and beginning to char. Transfer the peppers to a large bowl and cover with a plate. When cool enough to handle, peel off the skin, remove the seeds and stems, and slice into strips. Set aside. 3. Meanwhile, in a large bowl, combine the ground beef with the garlic, salt, and pepper. Shape the beef into 4 patties. 4. Lower the heat on the air fryer to 360°F (182°C). Arrange the burgers in a single layer in the basket of the air fryer. Pausing halfway through the cooking time to turn the burgers, air fry for 10 minutes, or until a thermometer inserted into the thickest part registers 160°F (71°C). 5. Top the burgers with the cheese slices and continue baking for a minute or two, just until the cheese has melted. Serve the burgers on a lettuce leaf topped with the roasted poblano peppers.

Per Serving:
Calories: 489 | fat: 35g | protein: 39g | carbs: 3g | fiber: 1g | sodium: 703mg

Italian Sausage and Cheese Meatballs

Prep time: 10 minutes | Cook time: 20 minutes | Serves 4

½ pound (227 g) bulk Italian sausage
½ pound (227 g) 85% lean ground beef
½ cup shredded sharp Cheddar

cheese
½ teaspoon onion powder
½ teaspoon garlic powder
½ teaspoon black pepper

1. In a large bowl, gently mix the sausage, ground beef, cheese, onion powder, garlic powder, and pepper until well combined. 2. Form the mixture into 16 meatballs. Place the meatballs in a single layer in the air fryer basket. Set the air fryer to 350°F (177°C) for 20 minutes, turning the meatballs halfway through the cooking time. Use a meat thermometer to ensure the meatballs have reached an internal temperature of 160°F / 71°C (medium).

Per Serving:
Calories: 379 | fat: 31g | protein: 22g | carbs: 1g | net carbs: 1g | fiber: 0g

Steaks with Walnut-Blue Cheese Butter

Prep time: 30 minutes | Cook time: 10 minutes | Serves 6

½ cup unsalted butter, at room temperature
½ cup crumbled blue cheese
2 tablespoons finely chopped walnuts
1 tablespoon minced fresh rosemary
1 teaspoon minced garlic
¼ teaspoon cayenne pepper
Sea salt and freshly ground black pepper, to taste
1½ pounds (680 g) New York strip steaks, at room temperature

1. In a medium bowl, combine the butter, blue cheese, walnuts, rosemary, garlic, and cayenne pepper and salt and black pepper to taste. Use clean hands to ensure that everything is well combined. Place the mixture on a sheet of parchment paper and form it into a log. Wrap it tightly in plastic wrap. Refrigerate for at least 2 hours or freeze for 30 minutes. 2. Season the steaks generously with salt and pepper. 3. Place the air fryer basket or grill pan in the air fryer. Set the air fryer to 400ºF (204ºC) and let it preheat for 5 minutes. 4. Place the steaks in the basket in a single layer and air fry for 5 minutes. Flip the steaks, and cook for 5 minutes more, until an instant-read thermometer reads 120ºF (49ºC) for medium-rare (or as desired). 5. Transfer the steaks to a plate. Cut the butter into pieces and place the desired amount on top of the steaks. Tent a piece of aluminum foil over the steaks and allow to sit for 10 minutes before serving. 6. Store any remaining butter in a sealed container in the refrigerator for up to 2 weeks.

Per Serving:
Calories: 283 | fat: 18g | protein: 30g | carbs: 1g | net carbs: 1g | fiber: 0g

Italian Sausage Links

Prep time: 10 minutes | Cook time: 24 minutes | Serves 4

1 bell pepper (any color), sliced
1 medium onion, sliced
1 tablespoon avocado oil
1 teaspoon Italian seasoning
Sea salt and freshly ground black pepper, to taste
1 pound (454 g) Italian sausage links

1. Place the bell pepper and onion in a medium bowl, and toss with the avocado oil, Italian seasoning, and salt and pepper to taste. 2. Set the air fryer to 400ºF (204ºC). Put the vegetables in the air fryer basket and cook for 12 minutes. 3. Push the vegetables to the side of the basket and arrange the sausage links in the bottom of the basket in a single layer. Spoon the vegetables over the sausages. Cook for 12 minutes, tossing halfway through, until an instant-read thermometer inserted into the sausage reads 160ºF (71ºC).

Per Serving:
Calories: 444 | fat: 39g | protein: 17g | carbs: 5g | net carbs: 4g | fiber: 1g

Saucy Beef Fingers

Prep time: 30 minutes | Cook time: 14 minutes | Serves 4

1½ pounds (680 g) sirloin steak
¼ cup red wine
¼ cup fresh lime juice
1 teaspoon garlic powder
1 teaspoon shallot powder
1 teaspoon celery seeds
1 teaspoon mustard seeds
Coarse sea salt and ground black pepper, to taste
1 teaspoon red pepper flakes
2 eggs, lightly whisked
1 cup Parmesan cheese
1 teaspoon paprika

1. Place the steak, red wine, lime juice, garlic powder, shallot powder, celery seeds, mustard seeds, salt, black pepper, and red pepper in a large ceramic bowl; let it marinate for 3 hours. 2. Tenderize the cube steak by pounding with a mallet; cut into 1-inch strips. 3. In a shallow bowl, whisk the eggs. In another bowl, mix the Parmesan cheese and paprika. 4. Dip the beef pieces into the whisked eggs and coat on all sides. Now, dredge the beef pieces in the Parmesan mixture. 5. Cook at 400ºF (204ºC) for 14 minutes, flipping halfway through the cooking time. 6. Meanwhile, make the sauce by heating the reserved marinade in a saucepan over medium heat; let it simmer until thoroughly warmed. Serve the steak fingers with the sauce on the side. Enjoy!

Per Serving:
Calories: 483 | fat: 29g | protein: 49g | carbs: 4g | fiber: 1g | sodium: 141mg

Garlic Butter Steak Bites

Prep time: 5 minutes | Cook time: 16 minutes | Serves 3

Oil, for spraying
1 pound (454 g) boneless steak, cut into 1-inch pieces
2 tablespoons olive oil
1 teaspoon Worcestershire
sauce
½ teaspoon granulated garlic
½ teaspoon salt
¼ teaspoon freshly ground black pepper

1. Preheat the air fryer to 400ºF (204ºC). Line the air fryer basket with parchment and spray lightly with oil. 2. In a medium bowl, combine the steak, olive oil, Worcestershire sauce, garlic, salt, and black pepper and toss until evenly coated. 3. Place the steak in a single layer in the prepared basket. You may have to work in batches, depending on the size of your air fryer. 4. Cook for 10 to 16 minutes, flipping every 3 to 4 minutes. The total cooking time will depend on the thickness of the meat and your preferred doneness. If you want it well done, it may take up to 5 additional minutes.

Per Serving:
Calories: 293| fat: 17g | protein: 32g | carbs: 1g | fiber: 0g | sodium: 494mg

Indian Mint and Chile Kebabs

Prep time: 30 minutes | Cook time: 15 minutes | Serves 4

1 pound (454 g) ground lamb	½ teaspoon ground turmeric
½ cup finely minced onion	½ teaspoon cayenne pepper
¼ cup chopped fresh mint	¼ teaspoon ground cardamom
¼ cup chopped fresh cilantro	¼ teaspoon ground cinnamon
1 tablespoon minced garlic	1 teaspoon kosher salt

1. In the bowl of a stand mixer fitted with the paddle attachment, combine the lamb, onion, mint, cilantro, garlic, turmeric, cayenne, cardamom, cinnamon, and salt. Mix on low speed until you have a sticky mess of spiced meat. If you have time, let the mixture stand at room temperature for 30 minutes (or cover and refrigerate for up to a day or two, until you're ready to make the kebabs). 2. Divide the meat into eight equal portions. Form each into a long sausage shape. Place the kebabs in a single layer in the air fryer basket. Set the air fryer to 350°F (177°C) for 10 minutes. Increase the air fryer temperature to 400°F (204°C) and cook for 3 to 4 minutes more to brown the kebabs. Use a meat thermometer to ensure the kebabs have reached an internal temperature of 160°F / 71°C (medium).

Per Serving:

Calories: 231 | fat: 14g | protein: 23g | carbs: 3g | fiber: 1g | sodium: 648mg

Mojito Lamb Chops

Prep time: 30 minutes | Cook time: 5 minutes | Serves 2

Marinade:	2 teaspoons fine sea salt
2 teaspoons grated lime zest	½ teaspoon ground black
½ cup lime juice	pepper
¼ cup avocado oil	4 (1-inch-thick) lamb chops
¼ cup chopped fresh mint	Sprigs of fresh mint, for garnish
leaves	(optional)
4 cloves garlic, roughly	Lime slices, for serving
chopped	(optional)

1. Make the marinade: Place all the ingredients for the marinade in a food processor or blender and purée until mostly smooth with a few small chunks. Transfer half of the marinade to a shallow dish and set the other half aside for serving. Add the lamb to the shallow dish, cover, and place in the refrigerator to marinate for at least 2 hours or overnight. 2. Spray the air fryer basket with avocado oil. Preheat the air fryer to 390°F (199°C). 3. Remove the chops from the marinade and place them in the air fryer basket. Air fry for 5 minutes, or until the internal temperature reaches 145°F (63°C) for medium doneness. 4. Allow the chops to rest for 10 minutes before serving with the rest of the marinade as a sauce. Garnish with fresh mint leaves and serve with lime slices, if desired. Best served fresh.

Per Serving:

Calories: 597 | fat: 43g | protein: 47g | carbs: 8g | net carbs: 7g | fiber: 1g

Parmesan-Crusted Pork Chops

Prep time: 5 minutes | Cook time: 12 minutes | Serves 4

1 large egg	½ teaspoon salt
½ cup grated Parmesan cheese	¼ teaspoon ground black
4 (4-ounce / 113-g) boneless	pepper
pork chops	

1. Whisk egg in a medium bowl and place Parmesan in a separate medium bowl. 2. Sprinkle pork chops on both sides with salt and pepper. Dip each pork chop into egg, then press both sides into Parmesan. 3. Place pork chops into ungreased air fryer basket. Adjust the temperature to 400°F (204°C) and air fry for 12 minutes, turning chops halfway through cooking. Pork chops will be golden and have an internal temperature of at least 145°F (63°C) when done. Serve warm.

Per Serving:

Calories: 218 | fat: 9g | protein: 32g | carbs: 1g | fiber: 0g | sodium: 372mg

London Broil with Herb Butter

Prep time: 30 minutes | Cook time: 20 to 25 minutes | Serves 4

1½ pounds (680 g) London	softened
broil top round steak	1 tablespoon chopped fresh
¼ cup olive oil	parsley
2 tablespoons balsamic vinegar	¼ teaspoon salt
1 tablespoon Worcestershire	¼ teaspoon dried ground
sauce	rosemary or thyme
4 cloves garlic, minced	¼ teaspoon garlic powder
Herb Butter:	Pinch of red pepper flakes
6 tablespoons unsalted butter,	

1. Place the beef in a gallon-size resealable bag. In a small bowl, whisk together the olive oil, balsamic vinegar, Worcestershire sauce, and garlic. Pour the marinade over the beef, massaging gently to coat, and seal the bag. Let sit at room temperature for an hour or refrigerate overnight. 2. To make the herb butter: In a small bowl, mix the butter with the parsley, salt, rosemary, garlic powder, and red pepper flakes until smooth. Cover and refrigerate until ready to use. 3. Preheat the air fryer to 400°F (204°C). 4. Remove the beef from the marinade (discard the marinade) and place the beef in the air fryer basket. Pausing halfway through the cooking time to turn the meat, air fry for 20 to 25 minutes, until a thermometer inserted into the thickest part indicates the desired doneness, 125°F / 52°C (rare) to 150°F / 66°C (medium). Let the beef rest for 10 minutes before slicing. Serve topped with the herb butter.

Per Serving:

Calories: 519 | fat: 38g | protein: 39g | carbs: 3g | net carbs: 3g | fiber: 0g

Bacon and Cheese Stuffed Pork Chops

Prep time: 10 minutes | Cook time: 12 minutes | Serves 4

½ ounce (14 g) plain pork rinds, finely crushed

½ cup shredded sharp Cheddar cheese

4 slices cooked sugar-free bacon, crumbled

4 (4-ounce / 113-g) boneless pork chops

½ teaspoon salt

¼ teaspoon ground black pepper

1. In a small bowl, mix pork rinds, Cheddar, and bacon. 2. Make a 3-inch slit in the side of each pork chop and stuff with ¼ pork rind mixture. Sprinkle each side of pork chops with salt and pepper. 3. Place pork chops into ungreased air fryer basket, stuffed side up. Adjust the temperature to 400ºF (204ºC) and air fry for 12 minutes. Pork chops will be browned and have an internal temperature of at least 145ºF (63ºC) when done. Serve warm.

Per Serving:
calorie: 366 | fat: 16g | protein: 51g | carbs: 0g | sugars: 0g | fiber: 0g | sodium: 531mg

Sausage and Cauliflower Arancini

Prep time: 30 minutes | Cook time: 28 to 32 minutes | Serves 6

Avocado oil spray

6 ounces (170 g) Italian sausage, casings removed

¼ cup diced onion

1 teaspoon minced garlic

1 teaspoon dried thyme

Sea salt and freshly ground black pepper, to taste

2½ cups cauliflower rice

3 ounces (85 g) cream cheese

4 ounces (113 g) Cheddar cheese, shredded

1 large egg

½ cup finely ground blanched almond flour

¼ cup finely grated Parmesan cheese

Keto-friendly marinara sauce, for serving

1. Spray a large skillet with oil and place it over medium-high heat. Once the skillet is hot, put the sausage in the skillet and cook for 7 minutes, breaking up the meat with the back of a spoon. 2. Reduce the heat to medium and add the onion. Cook for 5 minutes, then add the garlic, thyme, and salt and pepper to taste. Cook for 1 minute more. 3. Add the cauliflower rice and cream cheese to the skillet. Cook for 7 minutes, stirring frequently, until the cream cheese melts and the cauliflower is tender. 4. Remove the skillet from the heat and stir in the Cheddar cheese. Using a cookie scoop, form the mixture into 1½-inch balls. Place the balls on a parchment paper-lined baking sheet. Freeze for 30 minutes. 5. Place the egg in a shallow bowl and beat it with a fork. In a separate bowl, stir together the almond flour and Parmesan cheese. 6. Dip the cauliflower balls into the egg, then coat them with the almond flour mixture, gently pressing the mixture to the balls to adhere. 7. Set the air fryer to 400ºF (204ºC). Spray the cauliflower rice balls with oil, and arrange them in a single layer in the air fryer basket, working in batches if necessary. Air fry for 5 minutes. Flip the rice balls and spray them with more oil. Air fry for 3 to 7 minutes longer, until the balls are golden brown. 8. Serve warm with marinara sauce.

Per Serving:
Calories: 312 | fat: 26g | protein: 14g | carbs: 6g | net carbs: 4g | fiber: 2g

Onion Pork Kebabs

Prep time: 22 minutes | Cook time: 18 minutes | Serves 3

2 tablespoons tomato purée

½ fresh serrano, minced

⅓ teaspoon paprika

1 pound (454 g) pork, ground

½ cup green onions, finely chopped

3 cloves garlic, peeled and finely minced

1 teaspoon ground black pepper, or more to taste

1 teaspoon salt, or more to taste

1. Thoroughly combine all ingredients in a mixing dish. Then form your mixture into sausage shapes. 2. Cook for 18 minutes at 355ºF (179ºC). Mound salad on a serving platter, top with air-fried kebabs and serve warm. Bon appétit!

Per Serving:
Calories: 216 | fat: 6g | protein: 35g | carbs: 4g | fiber: 1g | sodium: 855mg

Cajun Bacon Pork Loin Fillet

Prep time: 30 minutes | Cook time: 20 minutes | Serves 6

1½ pounds (680 g) pork loin fillet or pork tenderloin

3 tablespoons olive oil

2 tablespoons Cajun spice mix

Salt, to taste

6 slices bacon

Olive oil spray

1. Cut the pork in half so that it will fit in the air fryer basket. 2. Place both pieces of meat in a resealable plastic bag. Add the oil, Cajun seasoning, and salt to taste, if using. Seal the bag and massage to coat all of the meat with the oil and seasonings. Marinate in the refrigerator for at least 1 hour or up to 24 hours. 3. Remove the pork from the bag and wrap 3 bacon slices around each piece. Spray the air fryer basket with olive oil spray. Place the meat in the air fryer. Set the air fryer to 350ºF (177ºC) for 15 minutes. Increase the temperature to 400ºF (204ºC) for 5 minutes. Use a meat thermometer to ensure the meat has reached an internal temperature of 145ºF (63ºC). 4. Let the meat rest for 10 minutes. Slice into 6 medallions and serve.

Per Serving:
Calories: 289 | fat: 19g | protein: 27g | carbs: 0g | net carbs: 0g | fiber: 0g

Sausage-Stuffed Peppers

Prep time: 15 minutes | Cook time: 28 to 30 minutes | Serves 6

Avocado oil spray	black pepper, to taste
8 ounces (227 g) Italian sausage, casings removed	1 cup keto-friendly marinara sauce
½ cup chopped mushrooms	3 bell peppers, halved and seeded
¼ cup diced onion	3 ounces (85 g) provolone cheese, shredded
1 teaspoon Italian seasoning	
Sea salt and freshly ground	

1. Spray a large skillet with oil and place it over medium-high heat. Add the sausage and cook for 5 minutes, breaking up the meat with a wooden spoon. Add the mushrooms, onion, and Italian seasoning, and season with salt and pepper. Cook for 5 minutes more. Stir in the marinara sauce and cook until heated through. 2. Scoop the sausage filling into the bell pepper halves. 3. Set the air fryer to 350°F (177°C). Arrange the peppers in a single layer in the air fryer basket, working in batches if necessary. Air fry for 15 minutes. 4. Top the stuffed peppers with the cheese and air fry for 3 to 5 minutes more, until the cheese is melted and the peppers are tender.

Per Serving:
Calories: 205 | fat: 16g | protein: 10g | carbs: 6g | net carbs: 5g | fiber: 1g

Tenderloin with Crispy Shallots

Prep time: 30 minutes | Cook time: 18 to 20 minutes | Serves 6

1½ pounds (680 g) beef tenderloin steaks	4 medium shallots
Sea salt and freshly ground black pepper, to taste	1 teaspoon olive oil or avocado oil

1. Season both sides of the steaks with salt and pepper, and let them sit at room temperature for 45 minutes. 2. Set the air fryer to 400°F (204°C) and let it preheat for 5 minutes. 3. Working in batches if necessary, place the steaks in the air fryer basket in a single layer and air fry for 5 minutes. Flip and cook for 5 minutes longer, until an instant-read thermometer inserted in the center of the steaks registers 120°F (49°C) for medium-rare (or as desired). Remove the steaks and tent with aluminum foil to rest. 4. Set the air fryer to 300°F (149°C). In a medium bowl, toss the shallots with the oil. Place the shallots in the basket and air fry for 5 minutes, then give them a toss and cook for 3 to 5 minutes more, until crispy and golden brown. 5. Place the steaks on serving plates and arrange the shallots on top.

Per Serving:
Calories: 166 | fat: 8g | protein: 24g | carbs: 1g | fiber: 0g | sodium: 72mg

Pork Milanese

Prep time: 10 minutes | Cook time: 12 minutes | Serves 4

4 (1-inch) boneless pork chops	cheese
Fine sea salt and ground black pepper, to taste	Chopped fresh parsley, for garnish
2 large eggs	Lemon slices, for serving
¾ cup powdered Parmesan	

1. Spray the air fryer basket with avocado oil. Preheat the air fryer to 400°F (204°C). 2. Place the pork chops between 2 sheets of plastic wrap and pound them with the flat side of a meat tenderizer until they're ¼ inch thick. Lightly season both sides of the chops with salt and pepper. 3. Lightly beat the eggs in a shallow bowl. Divide the Parmesan cheese evenly between 2 bowls and set the bowls in this order: Parmesan, eggs, Parmesan. Dredge a chop in the first bowl of Parmesan, then dip it in the eggs, and then dredge it again in the second bowl of Parmesan, making sure both sides and all edges are well coated. Repeat with the remaining chops. 4. Place the chops in the air fryer basket and air fry for 12 minutes, or until the internal temperature reaches 145°F (63°C), flipping halfway through. 5. Garnish with fresh parsley and serve immediately with lemon slices. Store leftovers in an airtight container in the refrigerator for up to 3 days. Reheat in a preheated 390°F (199°C) air fryer for 5 minutes, or until warmed through.

Per Serving:
Calories: 349 | fat: 14g | protein: 50g | carbs: 3g | fiber: 0g | sodium: 464mg

Mustard Lamb Chops

Prep time: 5 minutes | Cook time: 14 minutes | Serves 4

Oil, for spraying	
1 tablespoon Dijon mustard	¼ teaspoon freshly ground black pepper
2 teaspoons lemon juice	4 (1¼-inch-thick) loin lamb chops
½ teaspoon dried tarragon	
¼ teaspoon salt	

1. Preheat the air fryer to 390°F (199°C). Line the air fryer basket with parchment and spray lightly with oil. 2. In a small bowl, mix together the mustard, lemon juice, tarragon, salt, and black pepper. 3. Pat dry the lamb chops with a paper towel. Brush the chops on both sides with the mustard mixture. 4. Place the chops in the prepared basket. You may need to work in batches, depending on the size of your air fryer. 5. Cook for 8 minutes, flip, and cook for another 6 minutes, or until the internal temperature reaches 125°F (52°C) for rare, 145°F (63°C) for medium-rare, or 155°F (68°C) for medium.

Per Serving:
Calories: 96 | fat: 4g | protein: 14g | carbs: 0g | fiber: 0g | sodium: 233mg

Chorizo and Beef Burger

Prep time: 10 minutes | Cook time: 15 minutes | Serves 4

¾ pound (340 g) 80/20 ground beef

¼ pound (113 g) Mexican-style ground chorizo

¼ cup chopped onion

5 slices pickled jalapeños, chopped

2 teaspoons chili powder

1 teaspoon minced garlic

¼ teaspoon cumin

1. In a large bowl, mix all ingredients. Divide the mixture into four sections and form them into burger patties. 2. Place burger patties into the air fryer basket, working in batches if necessary. 3. Adjust the temperature to 375ºF (191ºC) and air fry for 15 minutes. 4. Flip the patties halfway through the cooking time. Serve warm.

Per Serving:

Calories: 270 | fat: 20g | protein: 21g | carbs: 2g | net carbs: 1g | fiber: 1g

Savory Sausage Cobbler

Prep time: 15 minutes | Cook time: 34 minutes | Serves 4

Filling:

1 pound (454 g) ground Italian sausage

1 cup sliced mushrooms

1 teaspoon fine sea salt

2 cups marinara sauce

Biscuits:

3 large egg whites

¾ cup blanched almond flour

1 teaspoon baking powder

¼ teaspoon fine sea salt

2½ tablespoons very cold unsalted butter, cut into ¼-inch pieces

Fresh basil leaves, for garnish

1. Preheat the air fryer to 400ºF (204ºC). 2. Place the sausage in a pie pan (or a pan that fits into your air fryer). Use your hands to break up the sausage and spread it evenly on the bottom of the pan. Place the pan in the air fryer and air fry for 5 minutes. 3. Remove the pan from the air fryer and use a fork or metal spatula to crumble the sausage more. Season the mushrooms with the salt and add them to the pie pan. Stir to combine the mushrooms and sausage, then return the pan to the air fryer and air fry for 4 minutes, or until the mushrooms are soft and the sausage is cooked through. 4. Remove the pan from the air fryer. Add the marinara sauce and stir well. Set aside. 5. Make the biscuits: Place the egg whites in a large mixing bowl or the bowl of a stand mixer. Using a hand mixer or stand mixer, whip the egg whites until stiff peaks form. 6. In a medium-sized bowl, whisk together the almond flour, baking powder, and salt, then cut in the butter. Gently fold the flour mixture into the egg whites with a rubber spatula. 7. Using a large spoon or ice cream scoop, spoon one-quarter of the dough on top of the sausage mixture, making sure the butter stays in separate clumps. Repeat with the remaining dough, spacing the biscuits about 1 inch apart. 8. Place the pan in the air fryer and cook for 5 minutes, then lower the heat to 325ºF (163ºC) and bake for another 15 to 20 minutes, until the biscuits are golden brown. Serve garnished with

fresh basil leaves. 9. Store leftovers in an airtight container in the refrigerator for up to 3 days. Reheat in a preheated 350ºF (177ºC) air fryer for 5 minutes, or until warmed through.

Per Serving:

Calories: 572 | fat: 49g | protein: 23g | carbs: 11g | net carbs: 7g | fiber: 4g

Herbed Lamb Steaks

Prep time: 30 minutes | Cook time: 15 minutes | Serves 4

½ medium onion

2 tablespoons minced garlic

2 teaspoons ground ginger

1 teaspoon ground cinnamon

1 teaspoon onion powder

1 teaspoon cayenne pepper

1 teaspoon salt

4 (6-ounce / 170-g) boneless lamb sirloin steaks

Oil, for spraying

1. In a blender, combine the onion, garlic, ginger, cinnamon, onion powder, cayenne pepper, and salt and pulse until the onion is minced. 2. Place the lamb steaks in a large bowl or zip-top plastic bag and sprinkle the onion mixture over the top. Turn the steaks until they are evenly coated. Cover with plastic wrap or seal the bag and refrigerate for 30 minutes. 3. Preheat the air fryer to 330ºF (166ºC). Line the air fryer basket with parchment and spray lightly with oil. 4. Place the lamb steaks in a single layer in the prepared basket, making sure they don't overlap. You may need to work in batches, depending on the size of your air fryer. 5. Cook for 8 minutes, flip, and cook for another 7 minutes, or until the internal temperature reaches 155ºF (68ºC).

Per Serving:

Calories: 255 | fat: 10g | protein: 35g | carbs: 5g | fiber: 1g | sodium: 720mg

Mexican-Style Shredded Beef

Prep time: 5 minutes | Cook time: 35 minutes | Serves 6

1 (2-pound / 907-g) beef chuck roast, cut into 2-inch cubes

1 teaspoon salt

½ teaspoon ground black

pepper

½ cup no-sugar-added chipotle sauce

1. In a large bowl, sprinkle beef cubes with salt and pepper and toss to coat. Place beef into ungreased air fryer basket. Adjust the temperature to 400ºF (204ºC) and air fry for 30 minutes, shaking the basket halfway through cooking. Beef will be done when internal temperature is at least 160ºF (71ºC). 2. Place cooked beef into a large bowl and shred with two forks. Pour in chipotle sauce and toss to coat. 3. Return beef to air fryer basket for an additional 5 minutes at 400ºF (204ºC) to crisp with sauce. Serve warm.

Per Serving:

Calories: 204 | fat: 9g | protein: 31g | carbs: 0g | fiber: 0g | sodium: 539mg

Ground Beef Taco Rolls

Prep time: 20 minutes | Cook time: 10 minutes | Serves 4

½ pound (227 g) 80/20 ground beef
⅓ cup water
1 tablespoon chili powder
2 teaspoons cumin
½ teaspoon garlic powder
¼ teaspoon dried oregano
¼ cup canned diced tomatoes and chiles, drained
2 tablespoons chopped cilantro
1½ cups shredded Mozzarella cheese
½ cup blanched finely ground almond flour
2 ounces (57 g) full-fat cream cheese
1 large egg

1. In a medium skillet over medium heat, brown the ground beef about 7 to 10 minutes. When meat is fully cooked, drain. 2. Add water to skillet and stir in chili powder, cumin, garlic powder, oregano, and tomatoes with chiles. Add cilantro. Bring to a boil, then reduce heat to simmer for 3 minutes. 3. In a large microwave-safe bowl, place Mozzarella, almond flour, cream cheese, and egg. Microwave for 1 minute. Stir the mixture quickly until smooth ball of dough forms. 4. Cut a piece of parchment for your work surface. Press the dough into a large rectangle on the parchment, wetting your hands to prevent the dough from sticking as necessary. Cut the dough into eight rectangles. 5. On each rectangle place a few spoons of the meat mixture. Fold the short ends of each roll toward the center and roll the length as you would a burrito. 6. Cut a piece of parchment to fit your air fryer basket. Place taco rolls onto the parchment and place into the air fryer basket. 7. Adjust the temperature to 360°F (182°C) and air fry for 10 minutes. 8. Flip halfway through the cooking time. 9. Allow to cool 10 minutes before serving.

Per Serving:
Calories: 411 | fat: 31g | protein: 27g | carbs: 7g | fiber: 3g | sodium: 176mg

MBaby Back Ribs

Prep time: 5 minutes | Cook time: 25 minutes | Serves 4

2 pounds (907 g) baby back ribs
2 teaspoons chili powder
1 teaspoon paprika
½ teaspoon onion powder
½ teaspoon garlic powder
¼ teaspoon ground cayenne pepper
½ cup low-carb, sugar-free barbecue sauce

1. Rub ribs with all ingredients except barbecue sauce. Place into the air fryer basket. 2. Adjust the temperature to 400°F (204°C) and roast for 25 minutes. 3. When done, ribs will be dark and charred with an internal temperature of at least 185°F (85°C). Brush ribs with barbecue sauce and serve warm.

Per Serving:
Calories: 571 | fat: 36g | protein: 45g | carbs: 17g | fiber: 1g | sodium: 541mg

Beef and Broccoli Stir-Fry

Prep time: 30 minutes | Cook time: 20 minutes | Serves 2

½ pound (227 g) sirloin steak, thinly sliced
2 tablespoons coconut aminos
¼ teaspoon grated ginger
¼ teaspoon finely minced garlic
1 tablespoon coconut oil
2 cups broccoli florets
¼ teaspoon crushed red pepper
⅛ teaspoon xanthan gum
½ teaspoon sesame seeds

1. To marinate beef, place it into a large bowl or storage bag and add coconut aminos, ginger, garlic, and coconut oil. Allow to marinate for 1 hour in refrigerator. 2. Remove beef from marinade, reserving marinade, and place beef into the air fryer basket. 3. Adjust the temperature to 320°F (160°C) and air fry for 20 minutes. 4. After 10 minutes, add broccoli and sprinkle red pepper into the basket and shake. 5. Pour the marinade into a skillet over medium heat and bring to a boil, then reduce to simmer. Stir in xanthan gum and allow to thicken. 6. When done, quickly empty fryer basket into skillet and toss. Sprinkle with sesame seeds. Serve immediately.

Per Serving:
Calories: 290 | fat: 20g | protein: 25g | carbs: 2g | net carbs: 1g | fiber: 1g

arinated Steak Tips with Mushrooms

Prep time: 30 minutes | Cook time: 10 minutes | Serves 4

1½ pounds (680 g) sirloin, trimmed and cut into 1-inch pieces
8 ounces (227 g) brown mushrooms, halved
¼ cup Worcestershire sauce
1 tablespoon Dijon mustard
1 tablespoon olive oil
1 teaspoon paprika
1 teaspoon crushed red pepper flakes
2 tablespoons chopped fresh parsley (optional)

1. Place the beef and mushrooms in a gallon-size resealable bag. In a small bowl, whisk together the Worcestershire, mustard, olive oil, paprika, and red pepper flakes. Pour the marinade into the bag and massage gently to ensure the beef and mushrooms are evenly coated. Seal the bag and refrigerate for at least 4 hours, preferably overnight. Remove from the refrigerator 30 minutes before cooking. 2. Preheat the air fryer to 400°F (204°C). 3. Drain and discard the marinade. Arrange the steak and mushrooms in the air fryer basket. Air fry for 10 minutes, pausing halfway through the baking time to shake the basket. Transfer to a serving plate and top with the parsley, if desired.

Per Serving:
Calories: 383 | fat: 23g | protein: 37g | carbs: 7g | fiber: 1g | sodium: 307mg

Bone-in Pork Chops

Prep time: 5 minutes | Cook time: 10 to 12 minutes | Serves 2

1 pound (454 g) bone-in pork chops

1 tablespoon avocado oil

1 teaspoon smoked paprika

½ teaspoon onion powder

¼ teaspoon cayenne pepper

Sea salt and freshly ground black pepper, to taste

1. Brush the pork chops with the avocado oil. In a small dish, mix together the smoked paprika, onion powder, cayenne pepper, and salt and black pepper to taste. Sprinkle the seasonings over both sides of the pork chops. 2. Set the air fryer to 400ºF (204ºC). Place the chops in the air fryer basket in a single layer, working in batches if necessary. Air fry for 10 to 12 minutes, until an instant-read thermometer reads 145ºF (63ºC) at the chops' thickest point. 3. Remove the chops from the air fryer and allow them to rest for 5 minutes before serving.

Per Serving:

Calories: 356 | fat: 16g | protein: 50g | carbs: 1g | fiber: 1g | sodium: 133mg

Mediterranean Beef Steaks

Prep time: 20 minutes | Cook time: 20 minutes | Serves 4

2 tablespoons coconut aminos

3 heaping tablespoons fresh chives

2 tablespoons olive oil

3 tablespoons dry white wine

4 small-sized beef steaks

2 teaspoons smoked cayenne pepper

½ teaspoon dried basil

½ teaspoon dried rosemary

1 teaspoon freshly ground black pepper

1 teaspoon sea salt, or more to taste

1. Firstly, coat the steaks with the cayenne pepper, black pepper, salt, basil, and rosemary. 2. Drizzle the steaks with olive oil, white wine, and coconut aminos. 3. Finally, roast in the air fryer for 20 minutes at 340ºF (171ºC). Serve garnished with fresh chives. Bon appétit!

Per Serving:

Calories: 320 | fat: 17g | protein: 37g | carbs: 5g | fiber: 1g | sodium: 401mg

Jalapeño Popper Pork Chops

Prep time: 15 minutes | Cook time: 6 to 8 minutes | Serves 4

1¾ pounds (794 g) bone-in, center-cut loin pork chops

Sea salt and freshly ground black pepper, to taste

6 ounces (170 g) cream cheese, at room temperature

4 ounces (113 g) sliced bacon, cooked and crumbled

4 ounces (113 g) Cheddar cheese, shredded

1 jalapeño, seeded and diced

1 teaspoon garlic powder

1. Cut a pocket into each pork chop, lengthwise along the side, making sure not to cut it all the way through. Season the outside of the chops with salt and pepper. 2. In a small bowl, combine the cream cheese, bacon, Cheddar cheese, jalapeño, and garlic powder. Divide this mixture among the pork chops, stuffing it into the pocket of each chop. 3. Set the air fryer to 400ºF (204ºC). Place the pork chops in the air fryer basket in a single layer, working in batches if necessary. Air fry for 3 minutes. Flip the chops and cook for 3 to 5 minutes more, until an instant-read thermometer reads 145ºF (63ºC). 4. Allow the chops to rest for 5 minutes, then serve warm.

Per Serving:

calorie: 469 | fat: 21g | protein: 60g | carbs: 5g | sugars: 3g | fiber: 0g | sodium: 576mg

Chapter 4 Poultry

Butter and Bacon Chicken

Prep time: 10 minutes | Cook time: 65 minutes | Serves 6

1 (4-pound / 1.8-kg) whole chicken
2 tablespoons salted butter, softened
1 teaspoon dried thyme
½ teaspoon garlic powder
1 teaspoon salt
½ teaspoon ground black pepper
6 slices sugar-free bacon

1. Pat chicken dry with a paper towel, then rub with butter on all sides. Sprinkle thyme, garlic powder, salt, and pepper over chicken. 2. Place chicken into ungreased air fryer basket, breast side up. Lay strips of bacon over chicken and secure with toothpicks. 3. Adjust the temperature to 350ºF (177ºC) and air fry for 65 minutes. Halfway through cooking, remove and set aside bacon and flip chicken over. Chicken will be done when the skin is golden and crispy and the internal temperature is at least 165ºF (74ºC). Serve warm with bacon.

Per Serving:
Calories: 563 | fat: 37g | protein: 56g | carbs: 1g | net carbs: 1g | fiber: 0g

Taco Chicken

Prep time: 10 minutes | Cook time: 23 minutes | Serves 4

2 large eggs
1 tablespoon water
Fine sea salt and ground black pepper, to taste
1 cup pork dust
1 teaspoon ground cumin
1 teaspoon smoked paprika
4 (5-ounce / 142-g) boneless,
skinless chicken breasts or thighs, pounded to ¼ inch thick
1 cup salsa
1 cup shredded Monterey Jack cheese (about 4 ounces / 113 g) (omit for dairy-free)
Sprig of fresh cilantro, for garnish (optional)

1. Spray the air fryer basket with avocado oil. Preheat the air fryer to 400ºF (204ºC). 2. Crack the eggs into a shallow baking dish, add the water and a pinch each of salt and pepper, and whisk to combine. In another shallow baking dish, stir together the pork dust, cumin, and paprika until well combined. 3. Season the chicken breasts well on both sides with salt and pepper. Dip 1 chicken breast in the eggs and let any excess drip off, then dredge both sides of the chicken breast in the pork dust mixture. Spray the breast with avocado oil and place it in the air fryer basket. Repeat with the remaining 3 chicken breasts. 4. Air fry the chicken in the air fryer for 20 minutes, or until the internal temperature reaches 165ºF (74ºC) and the breading is golden brown, flipping halfway through. 5. Dollop each chicken breast with ¼ cup of the salsa and top with ¼ cup of the cheese. Return the breasts to the air fryer and cook for 3 minutes, or until the cheese is melted. Garnish with cilantro before serving, if desired. 6. Store leftovers in an airtight container in the refrigerator for up to 4 days. Reheat in a preheated 400ºF (204ºC) air fryer for 5 minutes, or until warmed through.

Per Serving:
Calories: 360 | fat: 15g | protein: 20g | carbs: 4g | fiber: 1g | sodium: 490mg

Cilantro Chicken Kebabs

Prep time: 30 minutes | Cook time: 10 minutes | Serves 4

Chutney:
½ cup unsweetened shredded coconut
½ cup hot water
2 cups fresh cilantro leaves, roughly chopped
¼ cup fresh mint leaves, roughly chopped
6 cloves garlic, roughly chopped
1 jalapeño, seeded and roughly chopped
¼ to ¾ cup water, as needed
Juice of 1 lemon
Chicken:
1 pound (454 g) boneless, skinless chicken thighs, cut crosswise into thirds
Olive oil spray

1. For the chutney: In a blender or food processor, combine the coconut and hot water; set aside to soak for 5 minutes. 2. To the processor, add the cilantro, mint, garlic, and jalapeño, along with ¼ cup water. Blend at low speed, stopping occasionally to scrape down the sides. Add the lemon juice. With the blender or processor running, add only enough additional water to keep the contents moving. Turn the blender to high once the contents are moving freely and blend until the mixture is puréed. 3. For the chicken: Place the chicken pieces in a large bowl. Add ¼ cup of the chutney and mix well to coat. Set aside the remaining chutney to use as a dip. Marinate the chicken for 15 minutes at room temperature. 4. Spray the air fryer basket with olive oil spray. Arrange the chicken in the air fryer basket. Set the air fryer to 350ºF (177ºC) for 10 minutes. Use a meat thermometer to ensure that the chicken has reached an internal temperature of 165ºF (74ºC). 5. Serve the chicken with the remaining chutney.

Per Serving:
Calories: 184 | fat: 8g | protein: 23g | carbs: 4g | fiber: 1g | sodium: 115mg

Turkey Meatloaf

Prep time: 10 minutes | Cook time: 50 minutes | Serves 4

8 ounces (227 g) sliced mushrooms
1 small onion, coarsely chopped
2 cloves garlic
1½ pounds (680 g) 85% lean ground turkey
2 eggs, lightly beaten
1 tablespoon tomato paste
¼ cup almond meal
2 tablespoons almond milk
1 tablespoon dried oregano
1 teaspoon salt
½ teaspoon freshly ground black pepper
1 Roma tomato, thinly sliced

1. Preheat the air fryer to 350°F (177°C). Lightly coat a round pan with olive oil and set aside. 2. In a food processor fitted with a metal blade, combine the mushrooms, onion, and garlic. Pulse until finely chopped. Transfer the vegetables to a large mixing bowl. 3. Add the turkey, eggs, tomato paste, almond meal, milk, oregano, salt, and black pepper. Mix gently until thoroughly combined. Transfer the mixture to the prepared pan and shape into a loaf. Arrange the tomato slices on top. 4. Air fry for 50 minutes or until the meatloaf is nicely browned and a thermometer inserted into the thickest part registers 165°F (74°C). Remove from the air fryer and let rest for about 10 minutes before slicing.

Per Serving:
Calories: 353 | fat: 20g | protein: 38g | carbs: 7g | fiber: 2g | sodium: 625mg

Chicken Pesto Pizzas

Prep time: 10 minutes | Cook time: 12 minutes | Serves 4

1 pound (454 g) ground chicken thighs
¼ teaspoon salt
⅛ teaspoon ground black pepper
¼ cup basil pesto
1 cup shredded Mozzarella cheese
4 grape tomatoes, sliced

1. Cut four squares of parchment paper to fit into your air fryer basket. 2. Place ground chicken in a large bowl and mix with salt and pepper. Divide mixture into four equal sections. 3. Wet your hands with water to prevent sticking, then press each section into a 6-inch circle onto a piece of ungreased parchment. Place each chicken crust into air fryer basket, working in batches if needed. 4. Adjust the temperature to 350°F (177°C) and air fry for 10 minutes, turning crusts halfway through cooking. 5. Spread 1 tablespoon pesto across the top of each crust, then sprinkle with ¼ cup Mozzarella and top with 1 sliced tomato. Continue cooking at 350°F (177°C) for 2 minutes. Cheese will be melted and brown when done. Serve warm.

Per Serving:
Calories: 302 | fat: 18g | protein: 32g | carbs: 2g | fiber: 0g | sodium: 398mg

Jerk Chicken Thighs

Prep time: 30 minutes | Cook time: 15 to 20 minutes | Serves 6

2 teaspoons ground coriander
1 teaspoon ground allspice
1 teaspoon cayenne pepper
1 teaspoon ground ginger
1 teaspoon salt
1 teaspoon dried thyme
½ teaspoon ground cinnamon
½ teaspoon ground nutmeg
2 pounds (907 g) boneless chicken thighs, skin on
2 tablespoons olive oil

1. In a small bowl, combine the coriander, allspice, cayenne, ginger, salt, thyme, cinnamon, and nutmeg. Stir until thoroughly combined. 2. Place the chicken in a baking dish and use paper towels to pat dry. Thoroughly coat both sides of the chicken with the spice mixture. Cover and refrigerate for at least 2 hours, preferably overnight. 3. Preheat the air fryer to 360°F (182°C). 4. Working in batches if necessary, arrange the chicken in a single layer in the air fryer basket and lightly coat with the olive oil. Pausing halfway through the cooking time to flip the chicken, air fry for 15 to 20 minutes, until a thermometer inserted into the thickest part registers 165°F (74°C).

Per Serving:
Calories: 227 | fat: 11g | protein: 30g | carbs: 1g | fiber: 0g | sodium: 532mg

Ham Chicken with Cheese

Prep time: 15 minutes | Cook time: 25 minutes | Serves 4

¼ cup unsalted butter, softened
4 ounces (113 g) cream cheese, softened
1½ teaspoons Dijon mustard
2 tablespoons white wine vinegar
¼ cup water
2 cups shredded cooked chicken
¼ pound (113 g) ham, chopped
4 ounces (113 g) sliced Swiss or Provolone cheese

1. Preheat the air fryer to 380°F (193°C). Lightly coat a casserole dish that will fit in the air fryer, such as an 8-inch round pan, with olive oil and set aside. 2. In a large bowl and using an electric mixer, combine the butter, cream cheese, Dijon mustard, and vinegar. With the motor running at low speed, slowly add the water and beat until smooth. Set aside. 3. Arrange an even layer of chicken in the bottom of the prepared pan, followed by the ham. Spread the butter and cream cheese mixture on top of the ham, followed by the cheese slices on the top layer. Air fry for 20 to 25 minutes until warmed through and the cheese has browned.

Per Serving:
Calories: 509 | fat: 39g | protein: 35g | carbs: 2g | net carbs: 2g | fiber: 0g

Cajun-Breaded Chicken Bites

Prep time: 10 minutes | Cook time: 12 minutes | Serves 4

1 pound (454 g) boneless, skinless chicken breasts, cut into 1-inch cubes	pepper
	1 ounce (28 g) plain pork rinds, finely crushed
½ cup heavy whipping cream	¼ cup unflavored whey protein powder
½ teaspoon salt	
¼ teaspoon ground black	½ teaspoon Cajun seasoning

1. Place chicken in a medium bowl and pour in cream. Stir to coat. Sprinkle with salt and pepper. 2. In a separate large bowl, combine pork rinds, protein powder, and Cajun seasoning. Remove chicken from cream, shaking off any excess, and toss in dry mix until fully coated. 3. Place bites into ungreased air fryer basket. Adjust the temperature to 400°F (204°C) and air fry for 12 minutes, shaking the basket twice during cooking. Bites will be done when golden brown and have an internal temperature of at least 165°F (74°C). Serve warm.

Per Serving:
Calories: 272 | fat: 13g | protein: 35g | carbs: 2g | fiber: 1g | sodium: 513mg

Tandoori Chicken

Prep time: 30 minutes | Cook time: 15 minutes | Serves 4

1 pound (454 g) chicken tenders, halved crosswise	1 teaspoon ground turmeric
	1 teaspoon garam masala
¼ cup plain Greek yogurt	1 teaspoon sweet smoked paprika
1 tablespoon minced fresh ginger	
1 tablespoon minced garlic	1 tablespoon vegetable oil or melted ghee
¼ cup chopped fresh cilantro or parsley	
	2 teaspoons fresh lemon juice
1 teaspoon kosher salt	2 tablespoons chopped fresh cilantro
½ to 1 teaspoon cayenne pepper	

1. In a large glass bowl, toss together the chicken, yogurt, ginger, garlic, cilantro, salt, cayenne, turmeric, garam masala, and paprika to coat. Marinate at room temperature for 30 minutes, or cover and refrigerate for up to 24 hours. 2. Place the chicken in a single layer in the air fryer basket. (Discard remaining marinade.) Spray the chicken with oil. Set the air fryer to 350°F (177°C) for 15 minutes. Halfway through the cooking time, spray the chicken with more vegetable oil spray, and toss gently to coat. Cook for 5 minutes more. 3. Transfer the chicken to a serving platter. Sprinkle with lemon juice and toss to coat. Sprinkle with the cilantro and serve.

Per Serving:
Calories: 191 | fat: 9g | protein: 24g | carbs: 3g | net carbs: 2g | fiber: 1g

Greek Chicken Stir-Fry

Prep time: 15 minutes | Cook time: 15 minutes | Serves 2

1 (6-ounce / 170-g) chicken breast, cut into 1-inch cubes	and sliced
	1 tablespoon coconut oil
½ medium zucchini, chopped	1 teaspoon dried oregano
½ medium red bell pepper, seeded and chopped	½ teaspoon garlic powder
	¼ teaspoon dried thyme
¼ medium red onion, peeled	

1. Place all ingredients into a large mixing bowl and toss until the coconut oil coats the meat and vegetables. Pour the contents of the bowl into the air fryer basket. 2. Adjust the temperature to 375°F (191°C) and air fry for 15 minutes. 3. Shake the basket halfway through the cooking time to redistribute the food. Serve immediately.

Per Serving:
Calories: 183 | fat: 9g | protein: 20g | carbs: 4g | fiber: 1g | sodium: 44mg

Fried Chicken Breasts

Prep time: 30 minutes | Cook time: 12 to 14 minutes | Serves 4

1 pound (454 g) boneless, skinless chicken breasts	cheese
	½ teaspoon sea salt
¾ cup dill pickle juice	½ teaspoon freshly ground black pepper
¾ cup finely ground blanched almond flour	
	2 large eggs
¾ cup finely grated Parmesan	Avocado oil spray

1. Place the chicken breasts in a zip-top bag or between two pieces of plastic wrap. Using a meat mallet or heavy skillet, pound the chicken to a uniform ½-inch thickness. 2. Place the chicken in a large bowl with the pickle juice. Cover and allow to brine in the refrigerator for up to 2 hours. 3. In a shallow dish, combine the almond flour, Parmesan cheese, salt, and pepper. In a separate, shallow bowl, beat the eggs. 4. Drain the chicken and pat it dry with paper towels. Dip in the eggs and then in the flour mixture, making sure to press the coating into the chicken. Spray both sides of the coated breasts with oil. 5. Spray the air fryer basket with oil and put the chicken inside. Set the temperature to 400°F (204°C) and air fry for 6 to 7 minutes. 6. Carefully flip the breasts with a spatula. Spray the breasts again with oil and continue cooking for 6 to 7 minutes more, until golden and crispy.

Per Serving:
Calories: 319 | fat: 17g | protein: 37g | carbs: 5g | fiber: 3g | sodium: 399mg

Tex-Mex Chicken Roll-Ups

Prep time: 10 minutes | Cook time: 14 to 17 minutes | Serves 8

2 pounds (907 g) boneless, skinless chicken breasts or thighs
1 teaspoon chili powder
½ teaspoon smoked paprika
½ teaspoon ground cumin
Sea salt and freshly ground

black pepper, to taste
6 ounces (170 g) Monterey Jack cheese, shredded
4 ounces (113 g) canned diced green chiles
Avocado oil spray

1. Place the chicken in a large zip-top bag or between two pieces of plastic wrap. Using a meat mallet or heavy skillet, pound the chicken until it is about ¼ inch thick. 2. In a small bowl, combine the chili powder, smoked paprika, cumin, and salt and pepper to taste. Sprinkle both sides of the chicken with the seasonings. 3. Sprinkle the chicken with the Monterey Jack cheese, then the diced green chiles. 4. Roll up each piece of chicken from the long side, tucking in the ends as you go. Secure the roll-up with a toothpick. 5. Set the air fryer to 350ºF (177ºC). Spray the outside of the chicken with avocado oil. Place the chicken in a single layer in the basket, working in batches if necessary, and roast for 7 minutes. Flip and cook for another 7 to 10 minutes, until an instant-read thermometer reads 160ºF (71ºC). 6. Remove the chicken from the air fryer and allow it to rest for about 5 minutes before serving.

Per Serving:
Calories: 220 | fat: 10g | protein: 31g | carbs: 1g | fiber: 0g | sodium: 355mg

Blackened Cajun Chicken Tenders

Prep time: 10 minutes | Cook time: 17 minutes | Serves 4

2 teaspoons paprika
1 teaspoon chili powder
½ teaspoon garlic powder
½ teaspoon dried thyme
¼ teaspoon onion powder
⅛ teaspoon ground cayenne

pepper
2 tablespoons coconut oil
1 pound (454 g) boneless, skinless chicken tenders
¼ cup full-fat ranch dressing

1. In a small bowl, combine all seasonings. 2. Drizzle oil over chicken tenders and then generously coat each tender in the spice mixture. Place tenders into the air fryer basket. 3. Adjust the temperature to 375ºF (191ºC) and air fry for 17 minutes. 4. Tenders will be 165ºF (74ºC) internally when fully cooked. Serve with ranch dressing for dipping.

Per Serving:
Calories: 266 | fat: 17g | protein: 26g | carbs: 2g | fiber: 1g | sodium: 207mg

Ginger Turmeric Chicken Thighs

Prep time: 5 minutes | Cook time: 25 minutes | Serves 4

4 (4-ounce / 113-g) boneless, skin-on chicken thighs
2 tablespoons coconut oil, melted
½ teaspoon ground turmeric

½ teaspoon salt
½ teaspoon garlic powder
½ teaspoon ground ginger
¼ teaspoon ground black pepper

1. Place chicken thighs in a large bowl and drizzle with coconut oil. Sprinkle with remaining ingredients and toss to coat both sides of thighs. 2. Place thighs skin side up into ungreased air fryer basket. Adjust the temperature to 400ºF (204ºC) and air fry for 25 minutes. After 10 minutes, turn thighs. When 5 minutes remain, flip thighs once more. Chicken will be done when skin is golden brown and the internal temperature is at least 165ºF (74ºC). Serve warm.

Per Serving:
Calories: 392 | fat: 31g | protein: 25g | carbs: 1g | fiber: 0g | sodium: 412mg

Bacon Lovers' Stuffed Chicken

Prep time: 10 minutes | Cook time: 20 minutes | Serves 4

4 (5-ounce / 142-g) boneless, skinless chicken breasts, pounded to ¼ inch thick
2 (5.2-ounce / 147-g) packages Boursin cheese (or Kite Hill brand chive cream cheese style

spread, softened, for dairy-free)
8 slices thin-cut bacon or beef bacon
Sprig of fresh cilantro, for garnish (optional)

1. Spray the air fryer basket with avocado oil. Preheat the air fryer to 400ºF (204ºC). 2. Place one of the chicken breasts on a cutting board. With a sharp knife held parallel to the cutting board, make a 1-inch-wide incision at the top of the breast. Carefully cut into the breast to form a large pocket, leaving a ½-inch border along the sides and bottom. Repeat with the other 3 chicken breasts. 3. Snip the corner of a large resealable plastic bag to form a ¾-inch hole. Place the Boursin cheese in the bag and pipe the cheese into the pockets in the chicken breasts, dividing the cheese evenly among them. 4. Wrap 2 slices of bacon around each chicken breast and secure the ends with toothpicks. Place the bacon-wrapped chicken in the air fryer basket and air fry until the bacon is crisp and the chicken's internal temperature reaches 165ºF (74ºC), about 18 to 20 minutes, flipping after 10 minutes. Garnish with a sprig of cilantro before serving, if desired. 5. Store leftovers in an airtight container in the refrigerator for up to 4 days. Reheat in a preheated 400ºF (204ºC) air fryer for 5 minutes, or until warmed through.

Per Serving:
Calories: 634 | fat: 49g | protein: 43g | carbs: 3g | net carbs: 3g | fiber: 0g
J

Spice-Rubbed Chicken Thighs

Prep time: 10 minutes | Cook time: 25 minutes | Serves 4

4 (4-ounce / 113-g) bone-in, skin-on chicken thighs	2 teaspoons chili powder
½ teaspoon salt	1 teaspoon paprika
½ teaspoon garlic powder	1 teaspoon ground cumin
	1 small lime, halved

1. Pat chicken thighs dry and sprinkle with salt, garlic powder, chili powder, paprika, and cumin. 2. Squeeze juice from ½ lime over thighs. Place thighs into ungreased air fryer basket. Adjust the temperature to 380ºF (193ºC) and roast for 25 minutes, turning thighs halfway through cooking. Thighs will be crispy and browned with an internal temperature of at least 165ºF (74ºC) when done. 3. Transfer thighs to a large serving plate and drizzle with remaining lime juice. Serve warm.

Per Serving:
Calories: 151 | fat: 5g | protein: 23g | carbs: 3g | fiber: 1g | sodium: 439mg

Spinach and Feta Stuffed Chicken Breasts

Prep time: 10 minutes | Cook time: 27 minutes | Serves 4

1 (10-ounce / 283-g) package frozen spinach, thawed and drained well	black pepper
	4 boneless chicken breasts
1 cup feta cheese, crumbled	Salt and freshly ground black pepper, to taste
½ teaspoon freshly ground	1 tablespoon olive oil

1. Prepare the filling. Squeeze out as much liquid as possible from the thawed spinach. Rough chop the spinach and transfer it to a mixing bowl with the feta cheese and the freshly ground black pepper. 2. Prepare the chicken breast. Place the chicken breast on a cutting board and press down on the chicken breast with one hand to keep it stabilized. Make an incision about 1-inch long in the fattest side of the breast. Move the knife up and down inside the chicken breast, without poking through either the top or the bottom, or the other side of the breast. The inside pocket should be about 3-inches long, but the opening should only be about 1-inch wide. If this is too difficult, you can make the incision longer, but you will have to be more careful when cooking the chicken breast since this will expose more of the stuffing. 3. Once you have prepared the chicken breasts, use your fingers to stuff the filling into each pocket, spreading the mixture down as far as you can. 4. Preheat the air fryer to 380ºF (193ºC). 5. Lightly brush or spray the air fryer basket and the chicken breasts with olive oil. Transfer two of the stuffed chicken breasts to the air fryer. Air fry for 12 minutes, turning the chicken breasts over halfway through the cooking time. Remove the chicken to a resting plate and air fry the second two breasts for 12 minutes. Return the first batch of chicken to the air fryer with the second batch and air fry for 3 more minutes. When the chicken is cooked, an instant read thermometer should register 165ºF (74ºC)

in the thickest part of the chicken, as well as in the stuffing. 6. Remove the chicken breasts and let them rest on a cutting board for 2 to 3 minutes. Slice the chicken on the bias and serve with the slices fanned out.

Per Serving:
Calories: 476 | fat: 19g | protein: 69g | carbs: 5g | fiber: 2g | sodium: 519mg

Chicken Kiev

Prep time: 15 minutes | Cook time: 25 minutes | Serves 4

1 cup (2 sticks) unsalted butter, softened (or butter-flavored coconut oil for dairy-free)	1 teaspoon fine sea salt, divided
	4 (4-ounce / 113-g) boneless, skinless chicken breasts
2 tablespoons lemon juice	2 large eggs
2 tablespoons plus 1 teaspoon chopped fresh parsley leaves, divided, plus more for garnish	2 cups pork dust
	1 teaspoon ground black pepper
2 tablespoons chopped fresh tarragon leaves	Sprig of fresh parsley, for garnish
3 cloves garlic, minced	Lemon slices, for serving

1. Spray the air fryer basket with avocado oil. Preheat the air fryer to 350ºF (177ºC). 2. In a medium-sized bowl, combine the butter, lemon juice, 2 tablespoons of the parsley, the tarragon, garlic, and ¼ teaspoon of the salt. Cover and place in the fridge to harden for 7 minutes. 3. While the butter mixture chills, place one of the chicken breasts on a cutting board. With a sharp knife held parallel to the cutting board, make a 1-inch-wide incision at the top of the breast. Carefully cut into the breast to form a large pocket, leaving a ½-inch border along the sides and bottom. Repeat with the other 3 breasts. 4. Stuff one-quarter of the butter mixture into each chicken breast and secure the openings with toothpicks. 5. Beat the eggs in a small shallow dish. In another shallow dish, combine the pork dust, the remaining 1 teaspoon of parsley, the remaining ¾ teaspoon of salt, and the pepper. 6. One at a time, dip the chicken breasts in the egg, shake off the excess egg, and dredge the breasts in the pork dust mixture. Use your hands to press the pork dust onto each breast to form a nice crust. If you desire a thicker coating, dip it again in the egg and pork dust. As you finish, spray each coated chicken breast with avocado oil and place it in the air fryer basket. 7. Roast the chicken in the air fryer for 15 minutes, flip the breasts, and cook for another 10 minutes, or until the internal temperature of the chicken is 165ºF (74ºC) and the crust is golden brown. 8. Serve garnished with chopped fresh parsley and a parsley sprig, with lemon slices on the side. 9. Store leftovers in an airtight container in the refrigerator for up to 4 days or in the freezer for up to a month. Reheat in a preheated 350ºF (177ºC) air fryer for 5 minutes, or until heated through.

Per Serving:
Calories: 569 | fat: 40g | protein: 48g | carbs: 3g | net carbs: 3g | fiber: 0g

Broccoli Cheese Chicken

Prep time: 10 minutes | Cook time: 19 to 24 minutes | Serves 6

1 tablespoon avocado oil	additional for seasoning,
¼ cup chopped onion	divided
½ cup finely chopped broccoli	¼ freshly ground black pepper,
4 ounces (113 g) cream cheese,	plus additional for seasoning,
at room temperature	divided
2 ounces (57 g) Cheddar	2 pounds (907 g) boneless,
cheese, shredded	skinless chicken breasts
1 teaspoon garlic powder	1 teaspoon smoked paprika
½ teaspoon sea salt, plus	

1. Heat a medium skillet over medium-high heat and pour in the avocado oil. Add the onion and broccoli and cook, stirring occasionally, for 5 to 8 minutes, until the onion is tender. 2. Transfer to a large bowl and stir in the cream cheese, Cheddar cheese, and garlic powder, and season to taste with salt and pepper. 3. Hold a sharp knife parallel to the chicken breast and cut a long pocket into one side. Stuff the chicken pockets with the broccoli mixture, using toothpicks to secure the pockets around the filling. 4. In a small dish, combine the paprika, ½ teaspoon salt, and ¼ teaspoon pepper. Sprinkle this over the outside of the chicken. 5. Set the air fryer to 400ºF (204ºC). Place the chicken in a single layer in the air fryer basket, cooking in batches if necessary, and cook for 14 to 16 minutes, until an instant-read thermometer reads 160ºF (71ºC). Place the chicken on a plate and tent a piece of aluminum foil over the chicken. Allow to rest for 5 to 10 minutes before serving.

Per Serving:

calorie: 287 | fat: 16g | protein: 32g | carbs: 1g | sugars: 0g | fiber: 0g | sodium: 291mg

Smoky Chicken Leg Quarters

Prep time: 30 minutes | Cook time: 23 to 27 minutes | Serves 6

½ cup avocado oil	½ teaspoon dried thyme
2 teaspoons smoked paprika	½ teaspoon freshly ground
1 teaspoon sea salt	black pepper
1 teaspoon garlic powder	2 pounds (907 g) bone-in, skin-
½ teaspoon dried rosemary	on chicken leg quarters

1. In a blender or small bowl, combine the avocado oil, smoked paprika, salt, garlic powder, rosemary, thyme, and black pepper. 2. Place the chicken in a shallow dish or large zip-top bag. Pour the marinade over the chicken, making sure all the legs are coated. Cover and marinate for at least 2 hours or overnight. 3. Place the chicken in a single layer in the air fryer basket, working in batches if necessary. Set the air fryer to 400ºF (204ºC) and air fry for 15 minutes. Flip the chicken legs, then reduce the temperature to

350ºF (177ºC). Cook for 8 to 12 minutes more, until an instant-read thermometer reads 160ºF (71ºC) when inserted into the thickest piece of chicken. 4. Allow to rest for 5 to 10 minutes before serving.

Per Serving:

Calories: 347 | fat: 25g | protein: 29g | carbs: 1g | fiber: 0g | sodium: 534mg

Garlic Dill Wings

Prep time: 5 minutes | Cook time: 25 minutes | Serves 4

2 pounds (907 g) bone-in	pepper
chicken wings, separated at	½ teaspoon onion powder
joints	½ teaspoon garlic powder
½ teaspoon salt	1 teaspoon dried dill
½ teaspoon ground black	

1. In a large bowl, toss wings with salt, pepper, onion powder, garlic powder, and dill until evenly coated. Place wings into ungreased air fryer basket in a single layer, working in batches if needed. 2. Adjust the temperature to 400ºF (204ºC) and air fry for 25 minutes, shaking the basket every 7 minutes during cooking. Wings should have an internal temperature of at least 165ºF (74ºC) and be golden brown when done. Serve warm.

Per Serving:

Calories: 290 | fat: 8g | protein: 50g | carbs: 1g | fiber: 0g | sodium: 475mg

Ethiopian Chicken with Cauliflower

Prep time: 15 minutes | Cook time: 28 minutes | Serves 6

2 handful fresh Italian parsley,	⅓ teaspoon porcini powder
roughly chopped	1½teaspoons berbere spice
½ cup fresh chopped chives	⅓ teaspoon sweet paprika
2 sprigs thyme	½ teaspoon shallot powder
6 chicken drumsticks	1teaspoon granulated garlic
1½ small-sized head	1 teaspoon freshly cracked pink
cauliflower, broken into large-	peppercorns
sized florets	½ teaspoon sea salt
2 teaspoons mustard powder	

1. Simply combine all items for the berbere spice rub mix. After that, coat the chicken drumsticks with this rub mix on all sides. Transfer them to the baking dish. 2. Now, lower the cauliflower onto the chicken drumsticks. Add thyme, chives and Italian parsley and spritz everything with a pan spray. Transfer the baking dish to the preheated air fryer. 3. Next step, set the timer for 28 minutes; roast at 355ºF (179ºC), turning occasionally. Bon appétit!

Per Serving:

Calories: 235 | fat: 12g | protein: 25g | carbs: 5g | net carbs: 3g | fiber: 2g

Chicken Patties

Prep time: 15 minutes | Cook time: 12 minutes | Serves 4

1 pound (454 g) ground chicken thigh meat	½ teaspoon garlic powder
½ cup shredded Mozzarella cheese	¼ teaspoon onion powder
1 teaspoon dried parsley	1 large egg
	2 ounces (57 g) pork rinds, finely ground

1. In a large bowl, mix ground chicken, Mozzarella, parsley, garlic powder, and onion powder. Form into four patties. 2. Place patties in the freezer for 15 to 20 minutes until they begin to firm up. 3. Whisk egg in a medium bowl. Place the ground pork rinds into a large bowl. 4. Dip each chicken patty into the egg and then press into pork rinds to fully coat. Place patties into the air fryer basket. 5. Adjust the temperature to 360°F (182°C) and air fry for 12 minutes. 6. Patties will be firm and cooked to an internal temperature of 165°F (74°C) when done. Serve immediately.
Per Serving:
Calories: 265 | fat: 15g | protein: 29g | carbs: 1g | fiber: 0g | sodium: 285mg

Harissa-Rubbed Cornish Game Hens

Prep time: 30 minutes | Cook time: 21 minutes | Serves 4

Harissa:	1 teaspoon kosher salt
½ cup olive oil	½ to 1 teaspoon cayenne pepper
6 cloves garlic, minced	Hens:
2 tablespoons smoked paprika	½ cup yogurt
1 tablespoon ground coriander	2 Cornish game hens, any
1 tablespoon ground cumin	giblets removed, split in half
1 teaspoon ground caraway	lengthwise

1. For the harissa: In a medium microwave-safe bowl, combine the oil, garlic, paprika, coriander, cumin, caraway, salt, and cayenne. Microwave on high for 1 minute, stirring halfway through the cooking time. (You can also heat this on the stovetop until the oil is hot and bubbling. Or, if you must use your air fryer for everything, cook it in the air fryer at 350°F (177°C) for 5 to 6 minutes, or until the paste is heated through.) 2. For the hens: In a small bowl, combine 1 to 2 tablespoons harissa and the yogurt. Whisk until well combined. Place the hen halves in a resealable plastic bag and pour the marinade over. Seal the bag and massage until all of the pieces are thoroughly coated. Marinate at room temperature for 30 minutes or in the refrigerator for up to 24 hours. 3. Arrange the hen halves in a single layer in the air fryer basket. (If you have a smaller air fryer, you may have to cook this in two batches.) Set the air fryer to 400°F (204°C) for 20 minutes. Use a meat thermometer to ensure the game hens have reached an internal temperature of 165°F (74°C).
Per Serving:
Calories: 421 | fat: 33g | protein: 26g | carbs: 6g | fiber: 2g | sodium: 683mg

Chicken with Lettuce

Prep time: 15 minutes | Cook time: 14 minutes | Serves 4

1 pound (454 g) chicken breast tenders, chopped into bite-size pieces	thinly sliced
	1 tablespoon olive oil
½ onion, thinly sliced	1 tablespoon fajita seasoning
½ red bell pepper, seeded and thinly sliced	1 teaspoon kosher salt
	Juice of ½ lime
½ green bell pepper, seeded and	8 large lettuce leaves
	1 cup prepared guacamole

1. Preheat the air fryer to 400°F (204°C). 2. In a large bowl, combine the chicken, onion, and peppers. Drizzle with the olive oil and toss until thoroughly coated. Add the fajita seasoning and salt and toss again. 3. Working in batches if necessary, arrange the chicken and vegetables in a single layer in the air fryer basket. Pausing halfway through the cooking time to shake the basket, air fry for 14 minutes, or until the vegetables are tender and a thermometer inserted into the thickest piece of chicken registers 165°F (74°C). 4. Transfer the mixture to a serving platter and drizzle with the fresh lime juice. Serve with the lettuce leaves and top with the guacamole.
Per Serving:
Calories: 273 | fat: 15g | protein: 27g | carbs: 9g | fiber: 5g | sodium: 723mg

Chicken Thighs with Cilantro

Prep time: 15 minutes | Cook time: 25 minutes | Serves 4

1 tablespoon olive oil	8 bone-in chicken thighs, skin on
Juice of ½ lime	
1 tablespoon coconut aminos	2 tablespoons chopped fresh cilantro
1½ teaspoons Montreal chicken seasoning	

1. In a gallon-size resealable bag, combine the olive oil, lime juice, coconut aminos, and chicken seasoning. Add the chicken thighs, seal the bag, and massage the bag to ensure the chicken is thoroughly coated. Refrigerate for at least 2 hours, preferably overnight. 2. Preheat the air fryer to 400°F (204°C). 3. Remove the chicken from the marinade (discard the marinade) and arrange in a single layer in the air fryer basket. Pausing halfway through the cooking time to flip the chicken, air fry for 20 to 25 minutes, until a thermometer inserted into the thickest part registers 165°F (74°C). 4. Transfer the chicken to a serving platter and top with the cilantro before serving.
Per Serving:
Calories: 692 | fat: 53g | protein: 49g | carbs: 2g | fiber: 0g | sodium: 242mg

Thanksgiving Turkey Breast

Prep time: 5 minutes | Cook time: 30 minutes | Serves 4

1½ teaspoons fine sea salt	1 teaspoon chopped fresh thyme
1 teaspoon ground black pepper	leaves
1 teaspoon chopped fresh	1 (2-pound / 907-g) turkey
rosemary leaves	breast
1 teaspoon chopped fresh sage	3 tablespoons ghee or unsalted
1 teaspoon chopped fresh	butter, melted
tarragon	3 tablespoons Dijon mustard

1. Spray the air fryer with avocado oil. Preheat the air fryer to 390°F (199°C). 2. In a small bowl, stir together the salt, pepper, and herbs until well combined. Season the turkey breast generously on all sides with the seasoning. 3. In another small bowl, stir together the ghee and Dijon. Brush the ghee mixture on all sides of the turkey breast. 4. Place the turkey breast in the air fryer basket and air fry for 30 minutes, or until the internal temperature reaches 165°F (74°C). Transfer the breast to a cutting board and allow it to rest for 10 minutes before cutting it into ½-inch-thick slices. 5. Store leftovers in an airtight container in the refrigerator for up to 4 days or in the freezer for up to a month. Reheat in a preheated 350°F (177°C) air fryer for 4 minutes, or until warmed through.

Per Serving:

calorie: 418 | fat: 22g | protein: 51g | carbs: 1g | sugars: 0g | fiber: 1g | sodium: 603mg

Jerk Chicken Kebabs

Prep time: 10 minutes | Cook time: 14 minutes | Serves 4

8 ounces (227 g) boneless,	seeded and cut into 1-inch
skinless chicken thighs, cut into	pieces
1-inch cubes	¼ medium red onion, peeled
2 tablespoons jerk seasoning	and cut into 1-inch pieces
2 tablespoons coconut oil	½ teaspoon salt
½ medium red bell pepper,	

1. Place chicken in a medium bowl and sprinkle with jerk seasoning and coconut oil. Toss to coat on all sides. 2. Using eight (6-inch) skewers, build skewers by alternating chicken, pepper, and onion pieces, about three repetitions per skewer. 3. Sprinkle salt over skewers and place into ungreased air fryer basket. Adjust the temperature to 370°F (188°C) and air fry for 14 minutes, turning skewers halfway through cooking. Chicken will be golden and have an internal temperature of at least 165°F (74°C) when done. Serve warm.

Per Serving:

Calories: 142 | fat: 9g | protein: 12g | carbs: 4g | fiber: 1g | sodium: 348mg

Brazilian Tempero Baiano Chicken Drumsticks

Prep time: 30 minutes | Cook time: 20 minutes | Serves 4

1 teaspoon cumin seeds	½ teaspoon black peppercorns
1 teaspoon dried oregano	½ teaspoon cayenne pepper
1 teaspoon dried parsley	¼ cup fresh lime juice
1 teaspoon ground turmeric	2 tablespoons olive oil
½ teaspoon coriander seeds	1½ pounds (680 g) chicken
1 teaspoon kosher salt	drumsticks

1. In a clean coffee grinder or spice mill, combine the cumin, oregano, parsley, turmeric, coriander seeds, salt, peppercorns, and cayenne. Process until finely ground. 2. In a small bowl, combine the ground spices with the lime juice and oil. Place the chicken in a resealable plastic bag. Add the marinade, seal, and massage until the chicken is well coated. Marinate at room temperature for 30 minutes or in the refrigerator for up to 24 hours. 3. When you are ready to cook, place the drumsticks skin side up in the air fryer basket. Set the air fryer to 400°F (204°C) for 20 to 25 minutes, turning the legs halfway through the cooking time. Use a meat thermometer to ensure that the chicken has reached an internal temperature of 165°F (74°C). 4. Serve with plenty of napkins.

Per Serving:

Calories: 267 | fat: 13g | protein: 33g | carbs: 2g | fiber: 1g | sodium: 777mg

Classic Whole Chicken

Prep time: 5 minutes | Cook time: 50 minutes | Serves 4

Oil, for spraying	½ teaspoon salt
1 (4-pound / 1.8-kg) whole	½ teaspoon freshly ground
chicken, giblets removed	black pepper
1 tablespoon olive oil	¼ teaspoon finely chopped
1 teaspoon paprika	fresh parsley, for garnish
½ teaspoon granulated garlic	

1. Line the air fryer basket with parchment and spray lightly with oil. 2. Pat the chicken dry with paper towels. Rub it with the olive oil until evenly coated. 3. In a small bowl, mix together the paprika, garlic, salt, and black pepper and sprinkle it evenly over the chicken. 4. Place the chicken in the prepared basket, breast-side down. 5. Air fry at 360°F (182°C) for 30 minutes, flip, and cook for another 20 minutes, or until the internal temperature reaches 165°F (74°C) and the juices run clear. 6. Sprinkle with the parsley before serving.

Per Serving:

Calories: 549 | fat: 11g | protein: 105g | carbs: 0g | fiber: 0g | sodium: 523mg

Chicken and Broccoli Casserole

Prep time: 5 minutes | Cook time: 20 to 25 minutes | Serves 4

½ pound (227 g) broccoli, chopped into florets	½ teaspoon garlic powder
2 cups shredded cooked chicken	Salt and freshly ground black pepper, to taste
4 ounces (113 g) cream cheese	2 tablespoons chopped fresh basil
⅓ cup heavy cream	
1½ teaspoons Dijon mustard	1 cup shredded Cheddar cheese

1. Preheat the air fryer to 390ºF (199ºC). Lightly coat a casserole dish that will fit in air fryer, with olive oil and set aside. 2. Place the broccoli in a large glass bowl with 1 tablespoon of water and cover with a microwavable plate. Microwave on high for 2 to 3 minutes until the broccoli is bright green but not mushy. Drain if necessary and add to another large bowl along with the shredded chicken. 3. In the same glass bowl used to microwave the broccoli, combine the cream cheese and cream. Microwave for 30 seconds to 1 minute on high and stir until smooth. Add the mustard and garlic powder and season to taste with salt and freshly ground black pepper. Whisk until the sauce is smooth. 4. Pour the warm sauce over the broccoli and chicken mixture and then add the basil. Using a silicone spatula, gently fold the mixture until thoroughly combined. 5. Transfer the chicken mixture to the prepared casserole dish and top with the cheese. Air fry for 20 to 25 minutes until warmed through and the cheese has browned.

Per Serving:
Calories: 503 | fat: 39g | protein: 32g | carbs: 7g | fiber: 2g | sodium: 391mg

Thai Tacos with Peanut Sauce

Prep time: 10 minutes | Cook time: 6 minutes | Serves 4

1 pound (454 g) ground chicken	2 tablespoons wheat-free tamari or coconut aminos
¼ cup diced onions (about 1 small onion)	1½ teaspoons hot sauce
2 cloves garlic, minced	5 drops liquid stevia (optional)
¼ teaspoon fine sea salt	For Serving:
Sauce:	2 small heads butter lettuce, leaves separated
¼ cup creamy peanut butter, room temperature	Lime slices (optional)
2 tablespoons chicken broth, plus more if needed	For Garnish (Optional):
	Cilantro leaves
2 tablespoons lime juice	Shredded purple cabbage
2 tablespoons grated fresh ginger	Sliced green onions

1. Preheat the air fryer to 350ºF (177ºC). 2. Place the ground chicken, onions, garlic, and salt in a pie pan or a dish that will fit in your air fryer. Break up the chicken with a spatula. Place in the air fryer and bake for 5 minutes, or until the chicken is browned and cooked through. Break up the chicken again into small crumbles. 3. Make the sauce: In a medium-sized bowl, stir together the peanut butter, broth, lime juice, ginger, tamari, hot sauce, and stevia (if using) until well combined. If the sauce is too thick, add another tablespoon or two of broth. Taste and add more hot sauce if desired. 4. Add half of the sauce to the pan with the chicken. Cook for another minute, until heated through, and stir well to combine. 5. Assemble the tacos: Place several lettuce leaves on a serving plate. Place a few tablespoons of the chicken mixture in each lettuce leaf and garnish with cilantro leaves, purple cabbage, and sliced green onions, if desired. Serve the remaining sauce on the side. Serve with lime slices, if desired. 6. Store leftover meat mixture in an airtight container in the refrigerator for up to 4 days; store leftover sauce, lettuce leaves, and garnishes separately. Reheat the meat mixture in a lightly greased pie pan in a preheated 350ºF (177ºC) air fryer for 3 minutes, or until heated through.

Per Serving:
Calories: 276 | fat: 18g | protein: 25g | carbs: 5g | net carbs: 4g | fiber: 1g

Cobb Salad

Prep time: 15 minutes | Cook time: 8 minutes | Serves 4

8 slices reduced-sodium bacon	¼ cup almond milk
8 chicken breast tenders (about 1½ pounds / 680 g)	½ avocado
	Juice of ½ lime
8 cups chopped romaine lettuce	3 scallions, coarsely chopped
1 cup cherry tomatoes, halved	1 clove garlic
¼ red onion, thinly sliced	2 tablespoons fresh cilantro
2 hard-boiled eggs, peeled and sliced	⅛ teaspoon ground cumin
Avocado-Lime Dressing:	Salt and freshly ground black pepper, to taste
½ cup plain Greek yogurt	

1. Preheat the air fryer to 400ºF (204ºC). 2. Wrap a piece of bacon around each piece of chicken and secure with a toothpick. Working in batches if necessary, arrange the bacon-wrapped chicken in a single layer in the air fryer basket. Air fry for 8 minutes until the bacon is browned and a thermometer inserted into the thickest piece of chicken register 165ºF (74ºC). Let cool for a few minutes, then slice into bite-size pieces. 3. To make the dressing: In a blender or food processor, combine the yogurt, milk, avocado, lime juice, scallions, garlic, cilantro, and cumin. Purée until smooth. Season to taste with salt and freshly ground pepper. 4. To assemble the salad, in a large bowl, combine the lettuce, tomatoes, and onion. Drizzle the dressing over the vegetables and toss gently until thoroughly combined. Arrange the chicken and eggs on top just before serving.

Per Serving:
Calories: 630 | fat: 44g | protein: 48g | carbs: 10g | net carbs: 6g | fiber: 4g

Lemon Chicken

Prep time: 5 minutes | Cook time: 20 to 25 minutes | Serves 4

8 bone-in chicken thighs, skin on	½ teaspoon paprika
1 tablespoon olive oil	½ teaspoon garlic powder
1½ teaspoons lemon-pepper seasoning	¼ teaspoon freshly ground black pepper
	Juice of ½ lemon

1. Preheat the air fryer to 360°F (182°C). 2. Place the chicken in a large bowl and drizzle with the olive oil. Top with the lemon-pepper seasoning, paprika, garlic powder, and freshly ground black pepper. Toss until thoroughly coated. 3. Working in batches if necessary, arrange the chicken in a single layer in the basket of the air fryer. Pausing halfway through the cooking time to turn the chicken, air fry for 20 to 25 minutes, until a thermometer inserted into the thickest piece registers 165°F (74°C). 4. Transfer the chicken to a serving platter and squeeze the lemon juice over the top.

Per Serving:

Calories: 399 | fat: 19g | protein: 56g | carbs: 1g | fiber: 0g | sodium: 367mg

Chicken Pesto Parmigiana

Prep time: 10 minutes | Cook time: 23 minutes | Serves 4

2 large eggs	thighs, pounded to ¼ inch thick
1 tablespoon water	1 cup pesto
Fine sea salt and ground black pepper, to taste	1 cup shredded Mozzarella cheese (about 4 ounces / 113 g)
1 cup powdered Parmesan cheese (about 3 ounces / 85 g)	Finely chopped fresh basil, for garnish (optional)
2 teaspoons Italian seasoning	Grape tomatoes, halved, for serving (optional)
4 (5-ounce / 142-g) boneless, skinless chicken breasts or	

1. Spray the air fryer basket with avocado oil. Preheat the air fryer to 400°F (204°C). 2. Crack the eggs into a shallow baking dish, add the water and a pinch each of salt and pepper, and whisk to combine. In another shallow baking dish, stir together the Parmesan and Italian seasoning until well combined. 3. Season the chicken breasts well on both sides with salt and pepper. Dip one chicken breast in the eggs and let any excess drip off, then dredge both sides of the breast in the Parmesan mixture. Spray the breast with avocado oil and place it in the air fryer basket. Repeat with the remaining 3 chicken breasts. 4. Air fry the chicken in the air fryer for 20 minutes, or until the internal temperature reaches 165°F (74°C) and the breading is golden brown, flipping halfway through. 5. Dollop each chicken breast with ¼ cup of the pesto and top with the Mozzarella. Return the breasts to the air fryer and cook for 3 minutes, or until the cheese is melted. Garnish with basil and serve

with halved grape tomatoes on the side, if desired. 6. Store leftovers in an airtight container in the refrigerator for up to 4 days. Reheat in a preheated 400°F (204°C) air fryer for 5 minutes, or until warmed through.

Per Serving:

Calories: 631 | fat: 45g | protein: 52g | carbs: 4g | fiber: 0g | sodium: 607mg

Blackened Chicken

Prep time: 10 minutes | Cook time: 20 minutes | Serves 4

1 large egg, beaten	chicken breasts (about 1 pound / 454 g each), halved
¾ cup Blackened seasoning	1 to 2 tablespoons oil
2 whole boneless, skinless	

1. Place the beaten egg in one shallow bowl and the Blackened seasoning in another shallow bowl. 2. One at a time, dip the chicken pieces in the beaten egg and the Blackened seasoning, coating thoroughly. 3. Preheat the air fryer to 360°F (182°C). Line the air fryer basket with parchment paper. 4. Place the chicken pieces on the parchment and spritz with oil. 5. Cook for 10 minutes. Flip the chicken, spritz it with oil, and cook for 10 minutes more until the internal temperature reaches 165°F (74°C) and the chicken is no longer pink inside. Let sit for 5 minutes before serving.

Per Serving:

Calories: 225 | fat: 10g | protein: 28g | carbs: 8g | fiber: 6g | sodium: 512mg

Easy Turkey Tenderloin

Prep time: 20 minutes | Cook time: 30 minutes | Serves 4

Olive oil	black pepper
½ teaspoon paprika	Pinch cayenne pepper
½ teaspoon garlic powder	1½ pounds (680 g) turkey breast tenderloin
½ teaspoon salt	
½ teaspoon freshly ground	

1. Spray the air fryer basket lightly with olive oil. 2. In a small bowl, combine the paprika, garlic powder, salt, black pepper, and cayenne pepper. Rub the mixture all over the turkey. 3. Place the turkey in the air fryer basket and lightly spray with olive oil. 4. Air fry at 370°F (188°C) for 15 minutes. Flip the turkey over and lightly spray with olive oil. Air fry until the internal temperature reaches at least 170°F (77°C) for an additional 10 to 15 minutes. 5. Let the turkey rest for 10 minutes before slicing and serving.

Per Serving:

Calories: 196 | fat: 3g | protein: 40g | carbs: 1g | fiber: 0g | sodium: 483mg

Spice-Rubbed Turkey Breast

Prep time: 5 minutes | Cook time: 45 to 55 minutes | Serves 10

1 tablespoon sea salt	black pepper
1 teaspoon paprika	4 pounds (1.8 kg) bone-in, skin-
1 teaspoon onion powder	on turkey breast
1 teaspoon garlic powder	2 tablespoons unsalted butter,
½ teaspoon freshly ground	melted

1. In a small bowl, combine the salt, paprika, onion powder, garlic powder, and pepper. 2. Sprinkle the seasonings all over the turkey. Brush the turkey with some of the melted butter. 3. Set the air fryer to 350ºF (177ºC). Place the turkey in the air fryer basket, skin-side down, and roast for 25 minutes. 4. Flip the turkey and brush it with the remaining butter. Continue cooking for another 20 to 30 minutes, until an instant-read thermometer reads 160ºF (71ºC). 5. Remove the turkey breast from the air fryer. Tent a piece of aluminum foil over the turkey, and allow it to rest for about 5 minutes before serving.

Per Serving:

Calories: 302 | fat: 14g | protein: 40g | carbs: 1g | net carbs: 1g | fiber: 0g

French Garlic Chicken

Prep time: 30 minutes | Cook time: 27 minutes | Serves 4

2 tablespoon extra-virgin olive oil	1 teaspoon black pepper
1 tablespoon Dijon mustard	1 pound (454 g) boneless, skinless chicken thighs, halved
1 tablespoon apple cider vinegar	crosswise
3 cloves garlic, minced	2 tablespoons butter
2 teaspoons herbes de Provence	8 cloves garlic, chopped
½ teaspoon kosher salt	¼ cup heavy whipping cream

1. In a small bowl, combine the olive oil, mustard, vinegar, minced garlic, herbes de Provence, salt, and pepper. Use a wire whisk to emulsify the mixture. 2. Pierce the chicken all over with a fork to allow the marinade to penetrate better. Place the chicken in a resealable plastic bag, pour the marinade over, and seal. Massage until the chicken is well coated. Marinate at room temperature for 30 minutes or in the refrigerator for up to 24 hours. 3. When you are ready to cook, place the butter and chopped garlic in a baking pan and place it in the air fryer basket. Set the air fryer to 400ºF (204ºC) for 5 minutes, or until the butter has melted and the garlic is sizzling. 4. Add the chicken and the marinade to the seasoned butter. Set the air fryer to 350ºF (177ºC) for 15 minutes. Use a meat thermometer to ensure the chicken has reached an internal temperature of 165ºF (74ºC). Transfer the chicken to a plate and cover lightly with foil to keep warm. 5. Add the cream to the pan, stirring to combine with the garlic, butter, and cooking juices. Place the pan in the air fryer basket. Set the air fryer to 350ºF (177ºC) for 7 minutes. 6. Pour the thickened sauce over the chicken and serve.

Per Serving:

Calories: 291 | fat: 20g | protein: 23g | carbs: 4g | net carbs: 3g | fiber: 1g

Chipotle Aioli Wings

Prep time: 5 minutes | Cook time: 25 minutes | Serves 6

2 pounds (907 g) bone-in chicken wings	pepper
½ teaspoon salt	2 tablespoons mayonnaise
¼ teaspoon ground black	2 teaspoons chipotle powder
	2 tablespoons lemon juice

1. In a large bowl, toss wings in salt and pepper, then place into ungreased air fryer basket. Adjust the temperature to 400ºF (204ºC) and air fry for 25 minutes, shaking the basket twice while cooking. Wings will be done when golden and have an internal temperature of at least 165ºF (74ºC). 2. In a small bowl, whisk together mayonnaise, chipotle powder, and lemon juice. Place cooked wings into a large serving bowl and drizzle with aioli. Toss to coat. Serve warm.

Per Serving:

Calories: 210 | fat: 7g | protein: 34g | carbs: 1g | net carbs: 1g | fiber: 0g

Buffalo Chicken Cheese Sticks

Prep time: 5 minutes | Cook time: 8 minutes | Serves 2

1 cup shredded cooked chicken	cheese
¼ cup buffalo sauce	1 large egg
1 cup shredded Mozzarella	¼ cup crumbled feta

1. In a large bowl, mix all ingredients except the feta. Cut a piece of parchment to fit your air fryer basket and press the mixture into a ½-inch-thick circle. 2. Sprinkle the mixture with feta and place into the air fryer basket. 3. Adjust the temperature to 400ºF (204ºC) and air fry for 8 minutes. 4. After 5 minutes, flip over the cheese mixture. 5. Allow to cool 5 minutes before cutting into sticks. Serve warm.

Per Serving:

Calories: 413 | fat: 25g | protein: 43g | carbs: 3g | fiber: 0g | sodium: 453mg

Chicken Nuggets

Prep time: 10 minutes | Cook time: 15 minutes | Serves 4

1 pound (454 g) ground chicken thighs	1 large egg, whisked
½ cup shredded Mozzarella cheese	½ teaspoon salt
	¼ teaspoon dried oregano
	¼ teaspoon garlic powder

1. In a large bowl, combine all ingredients. Form mixture into twenty nugget shapes, about 2 tablespoons each. 2. Place nuggets into ungreased air fryer basket, working in batches if needed. Adjust the temperature to 375°F (191°C) and air fry for 15 minutes, turning nuggets halfway through cooking. Let cool 5 minutes before serving.

Per Serving:
Calories: 195 | fat: 8g | protein: 28g | carbs: 1g | fiber: 0g | sodium: 419mg

Nashville Hot Chicken

Prep time: 20 minutes | Cook time: 24 to 28 minutes | Serves 8

3 pounds (1.4 kg) bone-in, skin-on chicken pieces, breasts halved crosswise	divided
1 tablespoon sea salt	½ cup heavy (whipping) cream
1 tablespoon freshly ground black pepper	2 large eggs, beaten
1½ cups finely ground blanched almond flour	1 tablespoon vinegar-based hot sauce
1½ cups grated Parmesan cheese	Avocado oil spray
1 tablespoon baking powder	½ cup (1 stick) unsalted butter
2 teaspoons garlic powder,	½ cup avocado oil
	1 tablespoon cayenne pepper (more or less to taste)
	2 tablespoons Swerve

1. Sprinkle the chicken with the salt and pepper. 2. In a large shallow bowl, whisk together the almond flour, Parmesan cheese, baking powder, and 1 teaspoon of the garlic powder. 3. In a separate bowl, whisk together the heavy cream, eggs, and hot sauce. 4. Dip the chicken pieces in the egg, then coat each with the almond flour mixture, pressing the mixture into the chicken to adhere. Allow to sit for 15 minutes to let the breading set. 5. Set the air fryer to 400°F (204°C). Place the chicken in a single layer in the air fryer basket, being careful not to overcrowd the pieces, working in batches if

necessary. Spray the chicken with oil and roast for 13 minutes. 6. Carefully flip the chicken and spray it with more oil. Reduce the air fryer temperature to 350°F (177°C). Roast for another 11 to 15 minutes, until an instant-read thermometer reads 160°F (71°C). 7. While the chicken cooks, heat the butter, avocado oil, cayenne pepper, Swerve, and remaining 1 teaspoon of garlic powder in a saucepan over medium-low heat. Cook until the butter is melted and the sugar substitute has dissolved. 8. Remove the chicken from the air fryer. Use tongs to dip the chicken in the sauce. Place the coated chicken on a rack over a baking sheet, and allow it to rest for 5 minutes before serving.

Per Serving:
Calories: 693 | fat: 54g | protein: 46g | carbs: 7g | net carbs: 5g | fiber: 2g

Chipotle Drumsticks

Prep time: 5 minutes | Cook time: 25 minutes | Serves 4

1 tablespoon tomato paste	8 chicken drumsticks
½ teaspoon chipotle powder	½ teaspoon salt
¼ teaspoon apple cider vinegar	⅛ teaspoon ground black pepper
¼ teaspoon garlic powder	

1. In a small bowl, combine tomato paste, chipotle powder, vinegar, and garlic powder. 2. Sprinkle drumsticks with salt and pepper, then place into a large bowl and pour in tomato paste mixture. Toss or stir to evenly coat all drumsticks in mixture. 3. Place drumsticks into ungreased air fryer basket. Adjust the temperature to 400°F (204°C) and air fry for 25 minutes, turning drumsticks halfway through cooking. Drumsticks will be dark red with an internal temperature of at least 165°F (74°C) when done. Serve warm.

Per Serving:
Calories: 306 | fat: 10g | protein: 51g | carbs: 1g | fiber: 0g | sodium: 590mg

Chapter 5 Fish and Seafood

Cayenne Flounder Cutlets

Prep time: 15 minutes | Cook time: 10 minutes | Serves 2

1 egg	taste
1 cup Pecorino Romano cheese, grated	½ teaspoon cayenne pepper
	1 teaspoon dried parsley flakes
Sea salt and white pepper, to	2 flounder fillets

1. To make a breading station, whisk the egg until frothy. 2. In another bowl, mix Pecorino Romano cheese, and spices. 3. Dip the fish in the egg mixture and turn to coat evenly; then, dredge in the cracker crumb mixture, turning a couple of times to coat evenly. 4. Cook in the preheated air fryer at 390°F (199°C) for 5 minutes; turn them over and cook another 5 minutes. Enjoy!

Per Serving:
Calories: 280 | fat: 13g | protein: 36g | carbs: 3g | fiber: 1g | sodium: 257mg

Stuffed Flounder Florentine

Prep time: 10 minutes | Cook time: 25 minutes | Serves 4

¼ cup pine nuts	pepper, to taste
2 tablespoons olive oil	2 tablespoons unsalted butter, divided
½ cup chopped tomatoes	
1 (6-ounce / 170-g) bag spinach, coarsely chopped	4 flounder fillets (about 1½ pounds / 680 g)
2 cloves garlic, chopped	Dash of paprika
Salt and freshly ground black	½ lemon, sliced into 4 wedges

1. Place the pine nuts in a baking dish that fits in your air fryer. Set the air fryer to 400°F (204°C) and air fry for 4 minutes until the nuts are lightly browned and fragrant. Remove the baking dish from the air fryer, tip the nuts onto a plate to cool, and continue preheating the air fryer. When the nuts are cool enough to handle, chop them into fine pieces. 2. In the baking dish, combine the oil, tomatoes, spinach, and garlic. Use tongs to toss until thoroughly combined. Air fry for 5 minutes until the tomatoes are softened and the spinach is wilted. 3. Transfer the vegetables to a bowl and stir in the toasted pine nuts. Season to taste with salt and freshly ground black pepper. 4. Place 1 tablespoon of the butter in the bottom of the baking dish. Lower the heat on the air fryer to 350°F (177°C). 5. Place the flounder on a clean work surface. Sprinkle both sides with salt and black pepper. Divide the vegetable mixture among the flounder fillets and carefully roll up, securing with toothpicks. 6.

Working in batches if necessary, arrange the fillets seam-side down in the baking dish along with 1 tablespoon of water. Top the fillets with remaining 1 tablespoon butter and sprinkle with a dash of paprika. 7.Cover loosely with foil and air fry for 10 to 15 minutes until the fish is opaque and flakes easily with a fork. Remove the toothpicks before serving with the lemon wedges.

Per Serving:
Calories: 287 | fat: 21g | protein: 21g | carbs: 5g | sugars: 1g | fiber: 2g | sodium: 692mg

Crab-Stuffed Avocado Boats

Prep time: 5 minutes | Cook time: 7 minutes | Serves 4

2 medium avocados, halved and pitted	¼ teaspoon Old Bay seasoning
	2 tablespoons peeled and diced yellow onion
8 ounces (227 g) cooked crab meat	2 tablespoons mayonnaise

1. Scoop out avocado flesh in each avocado half, leaving ½ inch around edges to form a shell. Chop scooped-out avocado. 2. In a medium bowl, combine crab meat, Old Bay seasoning, onion, mayonnaise, and chopped avocado. Place ¼ mixture into each avocado shell. 3. Place avocado boats into ungreased air fryer basket. Adjust the temperature to 350°F (177°C) and air fry for 7 minutes. Avocado will be browned on the top and mixture will be bubbling when done. Serve warm.

Per Serving:
Calories: 226 | fat: 17g | protein: 12g | carbs: 10g | sugars: 1g | fiber: 7g | sodium: 239mg

Cod with Jalapeño

Prep time: 5 minutes | Cook time: 14 minutes | Serves 4

4 cod fillets, boneless	1 tablespoon avocado oil
1 jalapeño, minced	½ teaspoon minced garlic

1. In the shallow bowl, mix minced jalapeño, avocado oil, and minced garlic. 2. Put the cod fillets in the air fryer basket in one layer and top with minced jalapeño mixture. 3. Cook the fish at 365°F (185°C) for 7 minutes per side.

Per Serving:
Calories: 222 | fat: 5g | protein: 41g | carbs: 0g | fiber: 0g | sodium: 125mg

Snapper Scampi

Prep time: 5 minutes | Cook time: 8 to 10 minutes | Serves 4

4 (6-ounce / 170-g) skinless snapper or arctic char fillets	Pinch salt
1 tablespoon olive oil	Freshly ground black pepper, to taste
3 tablespoons lemon juice, divided	2 tablespoons butter
½ teaspoon dried basil	2 cloves garlic, minced

1. Rub the fish fillets with olive oil and 1 tablespoon of the lemon juice. Sprinkle with the basil, salt, and pepper, and place in the air fryer basket. 2. Air fry the fish at 380°F (193°C) for 7 to 8 minutes or until the fish just flakes when tested with a fork. Remove the fish from the basket and put on a serving plate. Cover to keep warm. 3. In a baking pan, combine the butter, remaining 2 tablespoons lemon juice, and garlic. Bake in the air fryer for 1 to 2 minutes or until the garlic is sizzling. Pour this mixture over the fish and serve

Per Serving:
Calories: 256 | fat: 11g | protein: 35g | carbs: 1g | net carbs: 1g | fiber: 0g

Salmon with Provolone Cheese

Prep time: 5 minutes | Cook time: 15 minutes | Serves 4

1 pound (454 g) salmon fillet, chopped	grated
2 ounces (57 g) Provolone,	1 teaspoon avocado oil
	¼ teaspoon ground paprika

1. Sprinkle the salmon fillets with avocado oil and put in the air fryer. 2. Then sprinkle the fish with ground paprika and top with Provolone cheese. 3. Cook the fish at 360°F (182°C) for 15 minutes.

Per Serving:
Calories: 204 | fat: 10g | protein: 27g | carbs: 0g | fiber: 0g | sodium: 209mg

Balsamic Tilapia

Prep time: 5 minutes | Cook time: 15 minutes | Serves 4

4 tilapia fillets, boneless	1 teaspoon avocado oil
2 tablespoons balsamic vinegar	1 teaspoon dried basil

1. Sprinkle the tilapia fillets with balsamic vinegar, avocado oil, and dried basil. 2. Then put the fillets in the air fryer basket and cook at 365°F (185°C) for 15 minutes.

Per Serving:
Calories: 129 | fat: 3g | protein: 23g | carbs: 1g | fiber: 0g | sodium: 92mg

Salmon Patties

Prep time: 5 minutes | Cook time: 8 minutes | Serves 4

12 ounces (340 g) pouched pink salmon	almond flour
3 tablespoons mayonnaise	½ teaspoon Cajun seasoning
⅓ cup blanched finely ground	1 medium avocado, peeled, pitted, and sliced

1. In a medium bowl, mix salmon, mayonnaise, flour, and Cajun seasoning. Form mixture into four patties. 2. Place patties into ungreased air fryer basket. Adjust the temperature to 400°F (204°C) and air fry for 8 minutes, turning patties halfway through cooking. Patties will be done when firm and golden brown. 3. Transfer patties to four medium plates and serve warm with avocado slices.

Per Serving:
Calories: 270 | fat: 19g | protein: 21g | carbs: 6g | net carbs: 1g | fiber: 5g

Coconut Cream Mackerel

Prep time: 10 minutes | Cook time: 6 minutes | Serves 4

2 pounds (907 g) mackerel fillet	1 teaspoon cumin seeds
1 cup coconut cream	1 garlic clove, peeled, chopped
1 teaspoon ground coriander	

1. Chop the mackerel roughly and sprinkle it with coconut cream, ground coriander, cumin seeds, and garlic. 2. Then put the fish in the air fryer and cook at 400°F (204°C) for 6 minutes.

Per Serving:
Calories: 439 | fat: 25g | protein: 48g | carbs: 4g | fiber: 1g | sodium: 362mg

Bacon-Wrapped Scallops

Prep time: 5 minutes | Cook time: 10 minutes | Serves 4

8 (1-ounce / 28-g) sea scallops, cleaned and patted dry	¼ teaspoon salt
8 slices sugar-free bacon	¼ teaspoon ground black pepper

1. Wrap each scallop in 1 slice bacon and secure with a toothpick. Sprinkle with salt and pepper. 2. Place scallops into ungreased air fryer basket. Adjust the temperature to 360°F (182°C) and air fry for 10 minutes. Scallops will be opaque and firm, and have an internal temperature of 135°F (57°C) when done. Serve warm.

Per Serving:
Calories: 251 | fat: 21g | protein: 13g | carbs: 2g | sugars: 0g | fiber: 0g | sodium: 612mg

Chilean Sea Bass with Olive Relish

Prep time: 10 minutes | Cook time: 10 minutes | Serves 2

Olive oil spray
2 (6-ounce / 170-g) Chilean sea bass fillets or other firm-fleshed white fish
3 tablespoons extra-virgin olive oil
½ teaspoon ground cumin
½ teaspoon kosher salt
½ teaspoon black pepper
⅓ cup pitted green olives, diced
¼ cup finely diced onion
1 teaspoon chopped capers

1. Spray the air fryer basket with the olive oil spray. Drizzle the fillets with the olive oil and sprinkle with the cumin, salt, and pepper. Place the fish in the air fryer basket. Set the air fryer to 325°F (163°C) for 10 minutes, or until the fish flakes easily with a fork. 2. Meanwhile, in a small bowl, stir together the olives, onion, and capers. 3. Serve the fish topped with the relish.

Per Serving:
Calories: 379 | fat: 26g | protein: 32g | carbs: 3g | fiber: 1g | sodium: 581mg

Breaded Shrimp Tacos

Prep time: 10 minutes | Cook time: 9 minutes |
Makes 8 tacos

2 large eggs
1 teaspoon prepared yellow mustard
1 pound (454 g) small shrimp, peeled, deveined, and tails removed
½ cup finely shredded Gouda or Parmesan cheese
½ cup pork dust
For Serving:
8 large Boston lettuce leaves
¼ cup pico de gallo
¼ cup shredded purple cabbage
1 lemon, sliced
Guacamole (optional)

1. Preheat the air fryer to 400°F (204°C). 2. Crack the eggs into a large bowl, add the mustard, and whisk until well combined. Add the shrimp and stir well to coat. 3. In a medium-sized bowl, mix together the cheese and pork dust until well combined. 4. One at a time, roll the coated shrimp in the pork dust mixture and use your hands to press it onto each shrimp. Spray the coated shrimp with avocado oil and place them in the air fryer basket, leaving space between them. 5. Air fry the shrimp for 9 minutes, or until cooked through and no longer translucent, flipping after 4 minutes. 6. To serve, place a lettuce leaf on a serving plate, place several shrimp on top, and top with 1½ teaspoons each of pico de gallo and purple cabbage. Squeeze some lemon juice on top and serve with guacamole, if desired. 7. Store leftover shrimp in an airtight container in the refrigerator for up to 3 days. Reheat in a preheated 400°F (204°C) air fryer for 5 minutes, or until warmed through.

Per Serving:
Calories: 115 | fat: 4g | protein: 18g | carbs: 2g | fiber: 1g | sodium: 253mg

Savory Shrimp

Prep time: 5 minutes | Cook time: 8 to 10 minutes |
Serves 4

1 pound (454 g) fresh large shrimp, peeled and deveined
1 tablespoon avocado oil
2 teaspoons minced garlic, divided
½ teaspoon red pepper flakes
Sea salt and freshly ground black pepper, to taste
2 tablespoons unsalted butter, melted
2 tablespoons chopped fresh parsley

1. Place the shrimp in a large bowl and toss with the avocado oil, 1 teaspoon of minced garlic, and red pepper flakes. Season with salt and pepper. 2. Set the air fryer to 350°F (177°C). Arrange the shrimp in a single layer in the air fryer basket, working in batches if necessary. Cook for 6 minutes. Flip the shrimp and cook for 2 to 4 minutes more, until the internal temperature of the shrimp reaches 120°F (49°C). (The time it takes to cook will depend on the size of the shrimp.) 3. While the shrimp are cooking, melt the butter in a small saucepan over medium heat and stir in the remaining 1 teaspoon of garlic. 4. Transfer the cooked shrimp to a large bowl, add the garlic butter, and toss well. Top with the parsley and serve warm.

Per Serving:
Calories: 182 | fat: 10g | protein: 23g | carbs: 1g | sugars: 0g | fiber: 0g | sodium: 127mg

Lemony Salmon

Prep time: 30 minutes | Cook time: 10 minutes | Serves 4

1½ pounds (680 g) salmon steak
½ teaspoon grated lemon zest
Freshly cracked mixed peppercorns, to taste
⅓ cup lemon juice
Fresh chopped chives, for garnish
½ cup dry white wine
½ teaspoon fresh cilantro, chopped
Fine sea salt, to taste

1. To prepare the marinade, place all ingredients, except for salmon steak and chives, in a deep pan. Bring to a boil over medium-high flame until it has reduced by half. Allow it to cool down. 2. After that, allow salmon steak to marinate in the refrigerator approximately 40 minutes. Discard the marinade and transfer the fish steak to the preheated air fryer. 3. Air fry at 400°F (204°C) for 9 to 10 minutes. To finish, brush hot fish steaks with the reserved marinade, garnish with fresh chopped chives, and serve right away!

Per Serving:
Calories: 244 | fat: 8g | protein: 35g | carbs: 3g | fiber: 0g | sodium: 128mg

Coconut Shrimp with Spicy Dipping Sauce

Prep time: 15 minutes | Cook time: 8 minutes | Serves 4

1 (2½-ounce / 71-g) bag pork rinds

¾ cup unsweetened shredded coconut flakes

¾ cup coconut flour

1 teaspoon onion powder

1 teaspoon garlic powder

2 eggs

1½ pounds (680 g) large

shrimp, peeled and deveined

½ teaspoon salt

¼ teaspoon freshly ground black pepper

Spicy Dipping Sauce:

½ cup mayonnaise

2 tablespoons Sriracha

Zest and juice of ½ lime

1 clove garlic, minced

1. Preheat the air fryer to 390ºF (199ºC). 2. In a food processor fitted with a metal blade, combine the pork rinds and coconut flakes. Pulse until the mixture resembles coarse crumbs. Transfer to a shallow bowl. 3. In another shallow bowl, combine the coconut flour, onion powder, and garlic powder; mix until thoroughly combined. 4. In a third shallow bowl, whisk the eggs until slightly frothy. 5. In a large bowl, season the shrimp with the salt and pepper, tossing gently to coat. 6. Working a few pieces at a time, dredge the shrimp in the flour mixture, followed by the eggs, and finishing with the pork rind crumb mixture. Arrange the shrimp on a baking sheet until ready to air fry. 7. Working in batches if necessary, arrange the shrimp in a single layer in the air fryer basket. Pausing halfway through the cooking time to turn the shrimp, air fry for 8 minutes until cooked through. 8. To make the sauce: In a small bowl, combine the mayonnaise, Sriracha, lime zest and juice, and garlic. Whisk until thoroughly combined. Serve alongside the shrimp.

Per Serving:

Calories: 473 | fat: 33g | protein: 30g | carbs: 13g | net carbs: 7g | fiber: 6g

Cajun Salmon

Prep time: 5 minutes | Cook time: 7 minutes | Serves 2

2 (4-ounce / 113-g) salmon fillets, skin removed

2 tablespoons unsalted butter, melted

⅛ teaspoon ground cayenne

pepper

½ teaspoon garlic powder

1 teaspoon paprika

¼ teaspoon ground black pepper

1. Brush each fillet with butter. 2. Combine remaining ingredients in a small bowl and then rub onto fish. Place fillets into the air fryer basket. 3. Adjust the temperature to 390ºF (199ºC) and air fry for 7 minutes. 4. When fully cooked, internal temperature will be 145ºF (63ºC). Serve immediately.

Per Serving:

Calories: 213 | fat: 12g | protein: 24g | carbs: 1g | net carbs: 0g | fiber: 1g

Shrimp Bake

Prep time: 15 minutes | Cook time: 5 minutes | Serves 4

14 ounces (397 g) shrimp, peeled

1 egg, beaten

½ cup coconut milk

1 cup Cheddar cheese, shredded

½ teaspoon coconut oil

1 teaspoon ground coriander

1. In the mixing bowl, mix shrimps with egg, coconut milk, Cheddar cheese, coconut oil, and ground coriander. 2. Then put the mixture in the baking ramekins and put in the air fryer. 3. Cook the shrimps at 400ºF (204ºC) for 5 minutes.

Per Serving:

Calories: 289 | fat: 19g | protein: 29g | carbs: 2g | net carbs: 1g | fiber: 1g

White Fish with Cauliflower

Prep time: 30 minutes | Cook time: 13 minutes | Serves 4

½ pound (227 g) cauliflower florets

½ teaspoon English mustard

2 tablespoons butter, room temperature

½ tablespoon cilantro, minced

2 tablespoons sour cream

2 ½ cups cooked white fish

Salt and freshly cracked black pepper, to taste

1. Boil the cauliflower until tender. Then, purée the cauliflower in your blender. Transfer to a mixing dish. 2. Now, stir in the fish, cilantro, salt, and black pepper. 3. Add the sour cream, English mustard, and butter; mix until everything's well incorporated. Using your hands, shape into patties. 4. Place in the refrigerator for about 2 hours. Cook for 13 minutes at 395ºF (202ºC). Serve with some extra English mustard.

Per Serving:

Calories: 297 | fat: 16g | protein: 33g | carbs: 5g | net carbs: 4g | fiber: 1g

Lime Lobster Tails

Prep time: 10 minutes | Cook time: 6 minutes | Serves 4

4 lobster tails, peeled

2 tablespoons lime juice

½ teaspoon dried basil

½ teaspoon coconut oil, melted

1. Mix lobster tails with lime juice, dried basil, and coconut oil. 2. Put the lobster tails in the air fryer and cook at 380ºF (193ºC) for 6 minutes.

Per Serving:

Calories: 123 | fat: 2g | protein: 25g | carbs: 1g | fiber: 0g | sodium: 635mg

Sesame-Crusted Tuna Steak

Prep time: 5 minutes | Cook time: 8 minutes | Serves 2

2 (6-ounce / 170-g) tuna steaks
1 tablespoon coconut oil, melted
½ teaspoon garlic powder
2 teaspoons white sesame seeds
2 teaspoons black sesame seeds

1. Brush each tuna steak with coconut oil and sprinkle with garlic powder. 2. In a large bowl, mix sesame seeds and then press each tuna steak into them, covering the steak as completely as possible. Place tuna steaks into the air fryer basket. 3. Adjust the temperature to 400°F (204°C) and air fry for 8 minutes. 4. Flip the steaks halfway through the cooking time. Steaks will be well-done at 145°F (63°C) internal temperature. Serve warm.

Per Serving:

Calories: 281 | fat: 11g | protein: 43g | carbs: 1g | fiber: 1g | sodium: 80mg

Lemon Mahi-Mahi

Prep time: 5 minutes | Cook time: 14 minutes | Serves 2

Oil, for spraying
2 (6-ounce / 170-g) mahi-mahi fillets
1 tablespoon lemon juice
1 tablespoon olive oil
¼ teaspoon salt
¼ teaspoon freshly ground black pepper
1 tablespoon chopped fresh dill
2 lemon slices

1. Line the air fryer basket with parchment and spray lightly with oil. 2. Place the mahi-mahi in the prepared basket. 3. In a small bowl, whisk together the lemon juice and olive oil. Brush the mixture evenly over the mahi-mahi. 4. Sprinkle the mahi-mahi with the salt and black pepper and top with the dill. 5. Air fry at 400°F (204°C) for 12 to 14 minutes, depending on the thickness of the fillets, until they flake easily. 6. Transfer to plates, top each with a lemon slice, and serve.

Per Serving:

Calories: 218 | fat: 8g | protein: 32g | carbs: 3g | fiber: 1g | sodium: 441mg

Fish Taco Bowl

Prep time: 10 minutes | Cook time: 12 minutes | Serves 4

½ teaspoon salt
¼ teaspoon garlic powder
¼ teaspoon ground cumin
4 (4-ounce / 113-g) cod fillets
4 cups finely shredded green cabbage
⅓ cup mayonnaise
¼ teaspoon ground black pepper
¼ cup chopped pickled jalapeños

1. Sprinkle salt, garlic powder, and cumin over cod and place into ungreased air fryer basket. Adjust the temperature to 350°F (177°C)

and air fry for 12 minutes, turning fillets halfway through cooking. Cod will flake easily and have an internal temperature of at least 145°F (63°C) when done. 2. In a large bowl, toss cabbage with mayonnaise, pepper, and jalapeños until fully coated. Serve cod warm over cabbage slaw on four medium plates.

Per Serving:

Calories: 161 | fat: 7g | protein: 19g | carbs: 5g | net carbs: 3g | fiber: 2g

Fish Fillets with Lemon-Dill Sauce

Prep time: 5 minutes | Cook time: 7 minutes | Serves 4

1 pound (454 g) snapper, grouper, or salmon fillets
Sea salt and freshly ground black pepper, to taste
1 tablespoon avocado oil
¼ cup sour cream
¼ cup sugar-free mayonnaise
2 tablespoons fresh dill, chopped, plus more for garnish
1 tablespoon freshly squeezed lemon juice
½ teaspoon grated lemon zest

1. Pat the fish dry with paper towels and season well with salt and pepper. Brush with the avocado oil. 2. Set the air fryer to 400°F (204°C). Place the fillets in the air fryer basket and air fry for 1 minute. 3. Lower the air fryer temperature to 325°F (163°C) and continue cooking for 5 minutes. Flip the fish and cook for 1 minute more or until an instant-read thermometer reads 145°F (63°C). (If using salmon, cook it to 125°F / 52°C for medium-rare.) 4. While the fish is cooking, make the sauce by combining the sour cream, mayonnaise, dill, lemon juice, and lemon zest in a medium bowl. Season with salt and pepper and stir until combined. Refrigerate until ready to serve. 5. Serve the fish with the sauce, garnished with the remaining dill.

Per Serving:

Calories: 223 | fat: 12g | protein: 25g | carbs: 4g | net carbs: 3g | fiber: 1g

Apple Cider Mussels

Prep time: 10 minutes | Cook time: 2 minutes | Serves 5

2 pounds (907 g) mussels, cleaned, peeled
1 teaspoon onion powder
1 teaspoon ground cumin
1 tablespoon avocado oil
¼ cup apple cider vinegar

1. Mix mussels with onion powder, ground cumin, avocado oil, and apple cider vinegar. 2. Put the mussels in the air fryer and cook at 395°F (202°C) for 2 minutes.

Per Serving:

Calories: 187 | fat: 7g | protein: 22g | carbs: 7g | fiber: 0g | sodium: 521mg

Southern-Style Catfish

Prep time: 10 minutes | Cook time: 12 minutes | Serves 4

4 (7-ounce / 198-g) catfish fillets	almond flour
⅓ cup heavy whipping cream	2 teaspoons Old Bay seasoning
1 tablespoon lemon juice	½ teaspoon salt
1 cup blanched finely ground	¼ teaspoon ground black pepper

1. Place catfish fillets into a large bowl with cream and pour in lemon juice. Stir to coat. 2. In a separate large bowl, mix flour and Old Bay seasoning. 3. Remove each fillet and gently shake off excess cream. Sprinkle with salt and pepper. Press each fillet gently into flour mixture on both sides to coat. 4. Place fillets into ungreased air fryer basket. Adjust the temperature to 400ºF (204ºC) and air fry for 12 minutes, turning fillets halfway through cooking. Catfish will be golden brown and have an internal temperature of at least 145ºF (63ºC) when done. Serve warm.

Per Serving:

Calories: 438 | fat: 28g | protein: 41g | carbs: 7g | fiber: 4g | sodium: 387mg

Friday Night Fish Fry

Prep time: 10 minutes | Cook time: 10 minutes | Serves 4

1 large egg	pepper
½ cup powdered Parmesan cheese (about 1½ ounces / 43 g)	4 (4-ounce / 113-g) cod fillets
1 teaspoon smoked paprika	Chopped fresh oregano or parsley, for garnish (optional)
¼ teaspoon celery salt	Lemon slices, for serving (optional)
¼ teaspoon ground black	

1. Spray the air fryer basket with avocado oil. Preheat the air fryer to 400ºF (204ºC). 2. Crack the egg in a shallow bowl and beat it lightly with a fork. Combine the Parmesan cheese, paprika, celery salt, and pepper in a separate shallow bowl. 3. One at a time, dip the fillets into the egg, then dredge them in the Parmesan mixture. Using your hands, press the Parmesan onto the fillets to form a nice crust. As you finish, place the fish in the air fryer basket. 4. Air fry the fish in the air fryer for 10 minutes, or until it is cooked through and flakes easily with a fork. Garnish with fresh oregano or parsley and serve with lemon slices, if desired. 5. Store leftovers in an airtight container in the refrigerator for up to 3 days. Reheat in a preheated 400ºF (204ºC) air fryer for 5 minutes, or until warmed through.

Per Serving:

Calories: 165 | fat: 6g | protein: 25g | carbs: 2g | fiber: 0g | sodium: 392mg

Paprika Crab Burgers

Prep time: 30 minutes | Cook time: 14 minutes | Serves 3

2 eggs, beaten	10 ounces (283 g) crab meat
1 shallot, chopped	1 teaspoon smoked paprika
2 garlic cloves, crushed	½ teaspoon ground black pepper
1 tablespoon olive oil	
1 teaspoon yellow mustard	Sea salt, to taste
1 teaspoon fresh cilantro, chopped	¾ cup Parmesan cheese

1. In a mixing bowl, thoroughly combine the eggs, shallot, garlic, olive oil, mustard, cilantro, crab meat, paprika, black pepper, and salt. Mix until well combined. 2. Shape the mixture into 6 patties. Roll the crab patties over grated Parmesan cheese, coating well on all sides. Place in your refrigerator for 2 hours. 3. Spritz the crab patties with cooking oil on both sides. Cook in the preheated air fryer at 360ºF (182ºC) for 14 minutes. Serve on dinner rolls if desired. Bon appétit!

Per Serving:

Calories: 288 | fat: 16g | protein: 32g | carbs: 4g | fiber: 1g | sodium: 355mg

Fish Gratin

Prep time: 30 minutes | Cook time: 17 minutes | Serves 4

1 tablespoon avocado oil	chopped
1 pound (454 g) hake fillets	½ cup Cottage cheese
1 teaspoon garlic powder	½ cup sour cream
Sea salt and ground white pepper, to taste	1 egg, well whisked
2 tablespoons shallots, chopped	1 teaspoon yellow mustard
1 bell pepper, seeded and	1 tablespoon lime juice
	½ cup Swiss cheese, shredded

1. Brush the bottom and sides of a casserole dish with avocado oil. Add the hake fillets to the casserole dish and sprinkle with garlic powder, salt, and pepper. 2. Add the chopped shallots and bell peppers. 3. In a mixing bowl, thoroughly combine the Cottage cheese, sour cream, egg, mustard, and lime juice. Pour the mixture over fish and spread evenly. 4. Cook in the preheated air fryer at 370ºF (188ºC) for 10 minutes. 5. Top with the Swiss cheese and cook an additional 7 minutes. Let it rest for 10 minutes before slicing and serving. Bon appétit!

Per Serving:

Calories: 256 | fat: 12g | protein: 28g | carbs: 8g | fiber: 1g | sodium: 523mg

Salmon with Cauliflower

Prep time: 10 minutes | Cook time: 25 minutes | Serves 4

1 pound (454 g) salmon fillet, diced

1 cup cauliflower, shredded

1 tablespoon dried cilantro

1 tablespoon coconut oil, melted

1 teaspoon ground turmeric

¼ cup coconut cream

1. Mix salmon with cauliflower, dried cilantro, ground turmeric, coconut cream, and coconut oil. 2. Transfer the salmon mixture into the air fryer and cook the meal at 350ºF (177ºC) for 25 minutes. Stir the meal every 5 minutes to avoid the burning.

Per Serving:

Calories: 232 | fat: 14g | protein: 24g | carbs: 3g | fiber: 1g | sodium: 94mg

Almond Catfish

Prep time: 10 minutes | Cook time: 12 minutes | Serves 4

2 pounds (907 g) catfish fillet

½ cup almond flour

2 eggs, beaten

1 teaspoon salt

1 teaspoon avocado oil

1. Sprinkle the catfish fillet with salt and dip in the eggs. 2. Then coat the fish in the almond flour and put in the air fryer basket. Sprinkle the fish with avocado oil. 3. Cook the fish for 6 minutes per side at 380ºF (193ºC).

Per Serving:

Calories: 308 | fat: 10g | protein: 42g | carbs: 11g | sugars: 0g | fiber: 2g | sodium: 610mg

Golden Shrimp

Prep time: 20 minutes | Cook time: 7 minutes | Serves 4

2 egg whites

½ cup coconut flour

1 cup Parmigiano-Reggiano, grated

½ teaspoon celery seeds

½ teaspoon porcini powder

½ teaspoon onion powder

1 teaspoon garlic powder

½ teaspoon dried rosemary

½ teaspoon sea salt

½ teaspoon ground black pepper

1½ pounds (680 g) shrimp, deveined

1. Whisk the egg with coconut flour and Parmigiano-Reggiano. Add in seasonings and mix to combine well. 2. Dip your shrimp in the batter. Roll until they are covered on all sides. 3. Cook in the preheated air fryer at 390ºF (199ºC) for 5 to 7 minutes or until golden brown. Work in batches. Serve with lemon wedges if desired.

Per Serving:

Calories: 265 | fat: 11g | protein: 33g | carbs: 7g | net carbs: 6g | fiber: 1g

Pecan-Crusted Catfish

Prep time: 5 minutes | Cook time: 12 minutes | Serves 4

½ cup pecan meal

1 teaspoon fine sea salt

¼ teaspoon ground black pepper

4 (4-ounce / 113-g) catfish

fillets

For Garnish (Optional):

Fresh oregano

Pecan halves

1. Spray the air fryer basket with avocado oil. Preheat the air fryer to 375ºF (191ºC). 2. In a large bowl, mix the pecan meal, salt, and pepper. One at a time, dredge the catfish fillets in the mixture, coating them well. Use your hands to press the pecan meal into the fillets. Spray the fish with avocado oil and place them in the air fryer basket. 3. Air fry the coated catfish for 12 minutes, or until it flakes easily and is no longer translucent in the center, flipping halfway through. 4. Garnish with oregano sprigs and pecan halves, if desired. 5. Store leftovers in an airtight container in the fridge for up to 3 days. Reheat in a preheated 350ºF (177ºC) air fryer for 4 minutes, or until heated through.

Per Serving:

Calories: 165 | fat: 3g | protein: 20g | carbs: 12g | fiber: 1g | sodium: 485mg

Tandoori Shrimp

Prep time: 25 minutes | Cook time: 6 minutes | Serves 4

1 pound (454 g) jumbo raw shrimp (21 to 25 count), peeled and deveined

1 tablespoon minced fresh ginger

3 cloves garlic, minced

¼ cup chopped fresh cilantro or parsley, plus more for garnish

1 teaspoon ground turmeric

1 teaspoon garam masala

1 teaspoon smoked paprika

1 teaspoon kosher salt

½ to 1 teaspoon cayenne pepper

2 tablespoons olive oil (for Paleo) or melted ghee

2 teaspoons fresh lemon juice

1. In a large bowl, combine the shrimp, ginger, garlic, cilantro, turmeric, garam masala, paprika, salt, and cayenne. Toss well to coat. Add the oil or ghee and toss again. Marinate at room temperature for 15 minutes, or cover and refrigerate for up to 8 hours. 2. Place the shrimp in a single layer in the air fryer basket. Set the air fryer to 325ºF (163ºC) for 6 minutes. Transfer the shrimp to a serving platter. Cover and let the shrimp finish cooking in the residual heat, about 5 minutes. 3. Sprinkle the shrimp with the lemon juice and toss to coat. Garnish with additional cilantro and serve.

Per Serving:

Calories: 167 | fat: 7g | protein: 23g | carbs: 2g | net carbs: 1g | fiber: 1g

Tilapia with Pecans

Prep time: 20 minutes | Cook time: 16 minutes | Serves 5

2 tablespoons ground flaxseeds	2 tablespoons extra-virgin olive
1 teaspoon paprika	oil
Sea salt and white pepper, to	½ cup pecans, ground
taste	5 tilapia fillets, sliced into
1 teaspoon garlic paste	halves

1. Combine the ground flaxseeds, paprika, salt, white pepper, garlic paste, olive oil, and ground pecans in a Ziploc bag. Add the fish fillets and shake to coat well. 2. Spritz the air fryer basket with cooking spray. Cook in the preheated air fryer at 400°F (204°C) for 10 minutes; turn them over and cook for 6 minutes more. Work in batches. 3. Serve with lemon wedges, if desired. Enjoy!

Per Serving:
Calories: 252 | fat: 17g | protein: 25g | carbs: 3g | fiber: 2g | sodium: 65mg

Mediterranean-Style Cod

Prep time: 5 minutes | Cook time: 12 minutes | Serves 4

4 (6-ounce / 170-g) cod fillets	6 cherry tomatoes, halved
3 tablespoons fresh lemon juice	¼ cup pitted and sliced
1 tablespoon olive oil	kalamata olives
¼ teaspoon salt	

1. Place cod into an ungreased round nonstick baking dish. Pour lemon juice into dish and drizzle cod with olive oil. Sprinkle with salt. Place tomatoes and olives around baking dish in between fillets. 2. Place dish into air fryer basket. Adjust the temperature to 350°F (177°C) and bake for 12 minutes, carefully turning cod halfway through cooking. Fillets will be lightly browned, easily flake, and have an internal temperature of at least 145°F (63°C) when done. Serve warm.

Per Serving:
Calories: 186 | fat: 5g | protein: 31g | carbs: 2g | fiber: 1g | sodium: 300mg

Tuna-Stuffed Tomatoes

Prep time: 5 minutes | Cook time: 5 minutes | Serves 2

2 medium beefsteak tomatoes, tops removed, seeded, membranes removed	2 tablespoons mayonnaise
	¼ teaspoon salt
	¼ teaspoon ground black
2 (2.6-ounce / 74-g) pouches tuna packed in water, drained	pepper
	2 teaspoons coconut oil
1 medium stalk celery, trimmed and chopped	¼ cup shredded mild Cheddar cheese

1. Scoop pulp out of each tomato, leaving ½-inch shell. 2. In a medium bowl, mix tuna, celery, mayonnaise, salt, and pepper. Drizzle with coconut oil. Spoon ½ mixture into each tomato and top each with 2 tablespoons Cheddar. 3. Place tomatoes into ungreased air fryer basket. Adjust the temperature to 320°F (160°C) and air fry for 5 minutes. Cheese will be melted when done. Serve warm.

Per Serving:
Calories: 232 | fat: 15g | protein: 20g | carbs: 6g | net carbs: 4g | fiber: 2g

Baked Monkfish

Prep time: 20 minutes | Cook time: 12 minutes | Serves 2

2 teaspoons olive oil	1 tablespoon coconut aminos
1 cup celery, sliced	2 tablespoons lime juice
2 bell peppers, sliced	Coarse salt and ground black
1 teaspoon dried thyme	pepper, to taste
½ teaspoon dried marjoram	1 teaspoon cayenne pepper
½ teaspoon dried rosemary	½ cup Kalamata olives, pitted
2 monkfish fillets	and sliced

1. In a nonstick skillet, heat the olive oil for 1 minute. Once hot, sauté the celery and peppers until tender, about 4 minutes. Sprinkle with thyme, marjoram, and rosemary and set aside. 2. Toss the fish fillets with the coconut aminos, lime juice, salt, black pepper, and cayenne pepper. Place the fish fillets in the lightly greased air fryer basket and bake at 390°F (199°C) for 8 minutes. 3. Turn them over, add the olives, and cook an additional 4 minutes. Serve with the sautéed vegetables on the side. Bon appétit!

Per Serving:
Calories: 263 | fat: 11g | protein: 27g | carbs: 13g | fiber: 5g | sodium: 332mg

Crispy Fish Sticks

Prep time: 15 minutes | Cook time: 10 minutes | Serves 4

1 ounce (28 g) pork rinds, finely ground	1 tablespoon coconut oil
	1 large egg
¼ cup blanched finely ground almond flour	1 pound (454 g) cod fillet, cut into ¾-inch strips
½ teaspoon Old Bay seasoning	

1. Place ground pork rinds, almond flour, Old Bay seasoning, and coconut oil into a large bowl and mix together. In a medium bowl, whisk egg. 2. Dip each fish stick into the egg and then gently press into the flour mixture, coating as fully and evenly as possible. Place fish sticks into the air fryer basket. 3. Adjust the temperature to 400°F (204°C) and air fry for 10 minutes or until golden. 4. Serve immediately.

Per Serving:
Calories: 223 | fat: 14g | protein: 21g | carbs: 2g | fiber: 1g | sodium: 390mg

Scallops in Lemon-Butter Sauce

Prep time: 10 minutes | Cook time: 6 minutes | Serves 2

8 large dry sea scallops (about ¾ pound / 340 g)
Salt and freshly ground black pepper, to taste
2 tablespoons olive oil
2 tablespoons unsalted butter, melted

2 tablespoons chopped flat-leaf parsley
1 tablespoon fresh lemon juice
2 teaspoons capers, drained and chopped
1 teaspoon grated lemon zest
1 clove garlic, minced

1. Preheat the air fryer to 400°F (204°C). 2. Use a paper towel to pat the scallops dry. Sprinkle lightly with salt and pepper. Brush with the olive oil. Arrange the scallops in a single layer in the air fryer basket. Pausing halfway through the cooking time to turn the scallops, air fry for about 6 minutes until firm and opaque. 3. Meanwhile, in a small bowl, combine the oil, butter, parsley, lemon juice, capers, lemon zest, and garlic. Drizzle over the scallops just before serving.

Per Serving:

Calories: 304 | fat: 22g | protein: 21g | carbs: 5g | net carbs: 4g | fiber: 1g

Asian Swordfish

Prep time: 10 minutes | Cook time: 6 to 11 minutes | Serves 4

4 (4-ounce / 113-g) swordfish steaks
½ teaspoon toasted sesame oil
1 jalapeño pepper, finely minced
2 garlic cloves, grated
1 tablespoon grated fresh ginger

½ teaspoon Chinese five-spice powder
⅛ teaspoon freshly ground black pepper
2 tablespoons freshly squeezed lemon juice

1. Place the swordfish steaks on a work surface and drizzle with the sesame oil. 2. In a small bowl, mix the jalapeño, garlic, ginger, five-spice powder, pepper, and lemon juice. Rub this mixture into the fish and let it stand for 10 minutes. 3. Roast the swordfish in the air fryer at 380°F (193°C) for 6 to 11 minutes, or until the swordfish reaches an internal temperature of at least 140°F (60°C) on a meat thermometer. Serve immediately.

Per Serving:

Calories: 175 | fat: 8g | protein: 22g | carbs: 2g | fiber: 0g | sodium: 93mg

Snapper with Shallot and Tomato

Prep time: 20 minutes | Cook time: 15 minutes | Serves 2

2 snapper fillets
1 shallot, peeled and sliced
2 garlic cloves, halved
1 bell pepper, sliced
1 small-sized serrano pepper, sliced
1 tomato, sliced

1 tablespoon olive oil
¼ teaspoon freshly ground black pepper
½ teaspoon paprika
Sea salt, to taste
2 bay leaves

1. Place two parchment sheets on a working surface. Place the fish in the center of one side of the parchment paper. 2. Top with the shallot, garlic, peppers, and tomato. Drizzle olive oil over the fish and vegetables. Season with black pepper, paprika, and salt. Add the bay leaves. 3. Fold over the other half of the parchment. Now, fold the paper around the edges tightly and create a half moon shape, sealing the fish inside. 4. Cook in the preheated air fryer at 390°F (199°C) for 15 minutes. Serve warm.

Per Serving:

Calories: 325 | fat: 10g | protein: 47g | carbs: 11g | fiber: 2g | sodium: 146mg

Tuna Steak

Prep time: 10 minutes | Cook time: 12 minutes | Serves 4

1 pound (454 g) tuna steaks, boneless and cubed
1 tablespoon mustard

1 tablespoon avocado oil
1 tablespoon apple cider vinegar

1. Mix avocado oil with mustard and apple cider vinegar. 2. Then brush tuna steaks with mustard mixture and put in the air fryer basket. 3. Cook the fish at 360°F (182°C) for 6 minutes per side.

Per Serving:

Calories: 197 | fat: 9g | protein: 27g | carbs: 0g | fiber: 0g | sodium: 87mg

Chapter 6 Vegetables and Sides

Parmesan Mushrooms

Prep time: 5 minutes | Cook time: 15 minutes | Serves 4

Oil, for spraying
1 pound (454 g) cremini mushrooms, stems trimmed
2 tablespoons olive oil
2 teaspoons granulated garlic
1 teaspoon dried onion soup

mix
½ teaspoon salt
¼ teaspoon freshly ground black pepper
⅓ cup grated Parmesan cheese, divided

1. Line the air fryer basket with parchment and spray lightly with oil. 2. In a large bowl, toss the mushrooms with the olive oil, garlic, onion soup mix, salt, and black pepper until evenly coated. 3. Place the mushrooms in the prepared basket. 4. Roast at 370ºF (188ºC) for 13 minutes. 5. Sprinkle half of the cheese over the mushrooms and cook for another 2 minutes. 6. Transfer the mushrooms to a serving bowl, add the remaining Parmesan cheese, and toss until evenly coated. Serve immediately.

Per Serving:
Calories: 89 | fat: 9g | protein: 5g | carbs: 7g | fiber: 1g | sodium: 451mg

Cheesy Cauliflower Tots

Prep time: 15 minutes | Cook time: 12 minutes |
Makes 16 tots

1 large head cauliflower
1 cup shredded Mozzarella cheese
½ cup grated Parmesan cheese

1 large egg
¼ teaspoon garlic powder
¼ teaspoon dried parsley
⅛ teaspoon onion powder

1. On the stovetop, fill a large pot with 2 cups water and place a steamer in the pan. Bring water to a boil. Cut the cauliflower into florets and place on steamer basket. Cover pot with lid. 2. Allow cauliflower to steam 7 minutes until fork tender. Remove from steamer basket and place into cheesecloth or clean kitchen towel and let cool. Squeeze over sink to remove as much excess moisture as possible. The mixture will be too soft to form into tots if not all the moisture is removed. Mash with a fork to a smooth consistency. 3. Put the cauliflower into a large mixing bowl and add Mozzarella, Parmesan, egg, garlic powder, parsley, and onion powder. Stir until fully combined. The mixture should be wet but easy to mold. 4. Take 2 tablespoons of the mixture and roll into tot shape. Repeat with remaining mixture. Place into the air fryer basket. 5. Adjust

the temperature to 320ºF (160ºC) and set the timer for 12 minutes. 6. Turn tots halfway through the cooking time. Cauliflower tots should be golden when fully cooked. Serve warm.

Per Serving:
2 tots: calories: 82 | fat: 3g | protein: 9g | carbs: 7g | fiber: 2g | sodium: 258mg

Spinach and Sweet Pepper Poppers

Prep time: 10 minutes | Cook time: 8 minutes |
Makes 16 poppers

4 ounces (113 g) cream cheese, softened
1 cup chopped fresh spinach leaves

½ teaspoon garlic powder
8 mini sweet bell peppers, tops removed, seeded, and halved lengthwise

1. In a medium bowl, mix cream cheese, spinach, and garlic powder. Place 1 tablespoon mixture into each sweet pepper half and press down to smooth. 2. Place poppers into ungreased air fryer basket. Adjust the temperature to 400ºF (204ºC) and air fry for 8 minutes. Poppers will be done when cheese is browned on top and peppers are tender-crisp. Serve warm.

Per Serving:
Calories: 31 | fat: 2g | protein: 1g | carbs: 3g | fiber: 0g | sodium: 34mg

Burger Bun for One

Prep time: 2 minutes | Cook time: 5 minutes | Serves 1

2 tablespoons salted butter, melted
¼ cup blanched finely ground almond flour

¼ teaspoon baking powder
⅛ teaspoon apple cider vinegar
1 large egg, whisked

1. Pour butter into an ungreased ramekin. Add flour, baking powder, and vinegar to ramekin and stir until combined. Add egg and stir until batter is mostly smooth. 2. Place ramekin into air fryer basket. Adjust the temperature to 350ºF (177ºC) and bake for 5 minutes. When done, the center will be firm and the top slightly browned. Let cool, about 5 minutes, then remove from ramekin and slice in half. Serve.

Per Serving:
Calories: 422| fat: 40g | protein: 14g | carbs: 8g | net carbs: 4g | fiber: 4g

Bacon-Wrapped Asparagus

Prep time: 10 minutes | Cook time: 10 minutes | Serves 4

8 slices reduced-sodium bacon, cut in half

16 thick (about 1 pound / 454

g) asparagus spears, trimmed of woody ends

1. Preheat the air fryer to 350ºF (177ºC). 2. Wrap a half piece of bacon around the center of each stalk of asparagus. 3. Working in batches, if necessary, arrange seam-side down in a single layer in the air fryer basket. Air fry for 10 minutes until the bacon is crisp and the stalks are tender.

Per Serving:
Calories: 214| fat: 20g | protein: 7g | carbs: 1g | net carbs: 1g | fiber: 0g

Roasted Eggplant

Prep time: 15 minutes | Cook time: 15 minutes | Serves 4

1 large eggplant

2 tablespoons olive oil

¼ teaspoon salt

½ teaspoon garlic powder

1. Remove top and bottom from eggplant. Slice eggplant into ¼-inch-thick round slices. 2. Brush slices with olive oil. Sprinkle with salt and garlic powder. Place eggplant slices into the air fryer basket. 3. Adjust the temperature to 390ºF (199ºC) and set the timer for 15 minutes. 4. Serve immediately.

Per Serving:
Calories: 95| fat: 7g | protein: 1g | carbs: 8g | net carbs: 4g | fiber: 4g

Parmesan Herb Focaccia Bread

Prep time: 10 minutes | Cook time: 10 minutes | Serves 6

1 cup shredded Mozzarella cheese

1 ounce (28 g) full-fat cream cheese

1 cup blanched finely ground almond flour

¼ cup ground golden flaxseed

¼ cup grated Parmesan cheese

½ teaspoon baking soda

2 large eggs

½ teaspoon garlic powder

¼ teaspoon dried basil

¼ teaspoon dried rosemary

2 tablespoons salted butter, melted and divided

1. Place Mozzarella, cream cheese, and almond flour into a large microwave-safe bowl and microwave for 1 minute. Add the flaxseed, Parmesan, and baking soda and stir until smooth ball forms. If the mixture cools too much, it will be hard to mix. Return to microwave for 10 to 15 seconds to rewarm if necessary. 2. Stir in eggs. You may need to use your hands to get them fully incorporated. Just keep stirring and they will absorb into the dough. 3. Sprinkle dough with garlic powder, basil, and rosemary and knead into dough. Grease a baking pan with 1 tablespoon melted

butter. Press the dough evenly into the pan. Place pan into the air fryer basket. 4. Adjust the temperature to 400ºF (204ºC) and bake for 10 minutes. 5. At 7 minutes, cover with foil if bread begins to get too dark. 6. Remove and let cool at least 30 minutes. Drizzle with remaining butter and serve.

Per Serving:
Calories: 281| fat: 22g | protein: 16g | carbs: 9g | net carbs: 4g | fiber: 5g

Broccoli with Sesame Dressing

Prep time: 5 minutes | Cook time: 10 minutes | Serves 4

6 cups broccoli florets, cut into bite-size pieces

1 tablespoon olive oil

¼ teaspoon salt

2 tablespoons sesame seeds

2 tablespoons rice vinegar

2 tablespoons coconut aminos

2 tablespoons sesame oil

½ teaspoon Swerve

¼ teaspoon red pepper flakes (optional)

1. Preheat the air fryer to 400ºF (204ºC). 2. In a large bowl, toss the broccoli with the olive oil and salt until thoroughly coated. 3. Transfer the broccoli to the air fryer basket. Pausing halfway through the cooking time to shake the basket, air fry for 10 minutes until the stems are tender and the edges are beginning to crisp. 4. Meanwhile, in the same large bowl, whisk together the sesame seeds, vinegar, coconut aminos, sesame oil, Swerve, and red pepper flakes (if using). 5. Transfer the broccoli to the bowl and toss until thoroughly coated with the seasonings. Serve warm or at room temperature.

Per Serving:
Calories: 133| fat: 13g | protein: 3g | carbs: 3g | net carbs: 1g | fiber: 2g

Sweet and Crispy Roasted Pearl Onions

Prep time: 5 minutes | Cook time: 18 minutes | Serves 3

1 (14½-ounce / 411-g) package frozen pearl onions (do not thaw)

2 tablespoons extra-virgin olive oil

2 tablespoons balsamic vinegar

2 teaspoons finely chopped fresh rosemary

½ teaspoon kosher salt

¼ teaspoon black pepper

1. In a medium bowl, combine the onions, olive oil, vinegar, rosemary, salt, and pepper until well coated. 2. Transfer the onions to the air fryer basket. Set the air fryer to 400ºF (204ºC) for 18 minutes, or until the onions are tender and lightly charred, stirring once or twice during the cooking time.

Per Serving:
Calories: 145 | fat: 9g | protein: 2g | carbs: 15g | fiber: 2g | sodium: 396mg

Green Bean Casserole

Prep time: 10 minutes | Cook time: 20 minutes | Serves 4

1 pound (454 g) fresh green beans, ends trimmed, strings removed, and chopped into 2-inch pieces
1 (8-ounce / 227-g) package sliced brown mushrooms
½ onion, sliced
1 clove garlic, minced

1 tablespoon olive oil
½ teaspoon salt
¼ teaspoon freshly ground black pepper
4 ounces (113 g) cream cheese
½ cup chicken stock
¼ teaspoon ground nutmeg
½ cup grated Cheddar cheese

1. Preheat the air fryer to 400°F (204°C). Coat a casserole dish with olive oil and set aside. 2. In a large bowl, combine the green beans, mushrooms, onion, garlic, olive oil, salt, and pepper. Toss until the vegetables are thoroughly coated with the oil and seasonings. 3. Transfer the mixture to the air fryer basket. Pausing halfway through the cooking time to shake the basket, air fry for 10 minutes until tender. 4. While the vegetables are cooking, in a 2-cup glass measuring cup, warm the cream cheese and chicken stock in the microwave on high for 1 to 2 minutes until the cream cheese is melted. Add the nutmeg and whisk until smooth. 5. Transfer the vegetables to the prepared casserole dish and pour the cream cheese mixture over the top. Top with the Cheddar cheese. Air fry for another 10 minutes until the cheese is melted and beginning to brown.

Per Serving:
Calories: 230 | fat: 18g | protein: 8g | carbs: 11g | fiber: 3g | sodium: 502mg

Sesame-Ginger Broccoli

Prep time: 10 minutes | Cook time: 15 minutes | Serves 4

3 tablespoons toasted sesame oil
2 teaspoons sesame seeds
1 tablespoon chili-garlic sauce
2 teaspoons minced fresh ginger

½ teaspoon kosher salt
½ teaspoon black pepper
1 (16-ounce / 454-g) package frozen broccoli florets (do not thaw)

1. In a large bowl, combine the sesame oil, sesame seeds, chili-garlic sauce, ginger, salt, and pepper. Stir until well combined. Add the broccoli and toss until well coated. 2. Arrange the broccoli in the air fryer basket. Set the air fryer to 325°F (163°C) for 15 minutes, or until the broccoli is crisp, tender, and the edges are lightly browned, gently tossing halfway through the cooking time.

Per Serving:
Calories: 143 | fat: 11g | protein: 4g | carbs: 9g | fiber: 4g | sodium: 385mg

Zucchini Fritters

Prep time: 10 minutes | Cook time: 10 minutes | Serves 4

2 zucchini, grated (about 1 pound / 454 g)
1 teaspoon salt
¼ cup almond flour
¼ cup grated Parmesan cheese
1 large egg

¼ teaspoon dried thyme
¼ teaspoon ground turmeric
¼ teaspoon freshly ground black pepper
1 tablespoon olive oil
½ lemon, sliced into wedges

1. Preheat the air fryer to 400°F (204°C). Cut a piece of parchment paper to fit slightly smaller than the bottom of the air fryer. 2. Place the zucchini in a large colander and sprinkle with the salt. Let sit for 5 to 10 minutes. Squeeze as much liquid as you can from the zucchini and place in a large mixing bowl. Add the almond flour, Parmesan, egg, thyme, turmeric, and black pepper. Stir gently until thoroughly combined. 3. Shape the mixture into 8 patties and arrange on the parchment paper. Brush lightly with the olive oil. Pausing halfway through the cooking time to turn the patties, air fry for 10 minutes until golden brown. Serve warm with the lemon wedges.

Per Serving:
Calories: 78 | fat: 6g | protein: 4g | carbs: 2g | fiber: 0g | sodium: 712mg

Air-Fried Okra

Prep time: 10 minutes | Cook time: 10 minutes | Serves 4

1 egg
½ cup almond milk
½ cup crushed pork rinds
¼ cup grated Parmesan cheese
¼ cup almond flour
1 teaspoon garlic powder

¼ teaspoon freshly ground black pepper
½ pound (227 g) fresh okra, stems removed and chopped into 1-inch slices

1. Preheat the air fryer to 400°F (204°C). 2. In a shallow bowl, whisk together the egg and milk. 3. In a second shallow bowl, combine the pork rinds, Parmesan, almond flour, garlic powder, and black pepper. 4. Working with a few slices at a time, dip the okra into the egg mixture followed by the crumb mixture. Press lightly to ensure an even coating. 5. Working in batches if necessary, arrange the okra in a single layer in the air fryer basket and spray lightly with olive oil. Pausing halfway through the cooking time to turn the okra, air fry for 10 minutes until tender and golden brown. Serve warm.

Per Serving:
Calories: 200 | fat: 16g | protein: 6g | carbs: 8g | fiber: 2g | sodium: 228mg

Parmesan-Rosemary Radishes

Prep time: 5 minutes | Cook time: 15 to 20 minutes |
Serves 4

1 bunch radishes, stemmed, trimmed, and quartered	1 tablespoon chopped fresh rosemary
1 tablespoon avocado oil	Sea salt and freshly ground black pepper, to taste
2 tablespoons finely grated fresh Parmesan cheese	

1. Place the radishes in a medium bowl and toss them with the avocado oil, Parmesan cheese, rosemary, salt, and pepper. 2. Set the air fryer to 375ºF (191ºC). Arrange the radishes in a single layer in the air fryer basket. Roast for 15 to 20 minutes, until golden brown and tender. Let cool for 5 minutes before serving.

Per Serving:
Calories: 58 | fat: 4g | protein: 1g | carbs: 4g | fiber: 2g | sodium: 63mg

Garlic Roasted Broccoli

Prep time: 8 minutes | Cook time: 10 to 14 minutes |
Serves 6

1 head broccoli, cut into bite-size florets	Sea salt and freshly ground black pepper, to taste
1 tablespoon avocado oil	1 tablespoon freshly squeezed lemon juice
2 teaspoons minced garlic	½ teaspoon lemon zest
⅛ teaspoon red pepper flakes	

1. In a large bowl, toss together the broccoli, avocado oil, garlic, red pepper flakes, salt, and pepper. 2. Set the air fryer to 375ºF (191ºC). Arrange the broccoli in a single layer in the air fryer basket, working in batches if necessary. Roast for 10 to 14 minutes, until the broccoli is lightly charred. 3. Place the florets in a medium bowl and toss with the lemon juice and lemon zest. Serve.

Per Serving:
Calories: 58 | fat: 3g | protein: 3g | carbs: 7g | fiber: 3g | sodium: 34mg

Lemon-Thyme Asparagus

Prep time: 5 minutes | Cook time: 4 to 8 minutes |
Serves 4

1 pound (454 g) asparagus, woody ends trimmed off	black pepper, to taste
1 tablespoon avocado oil	2 ounces (57 g) goat cheese, crumbled
½ teaspoon dried thyme or ½ tablespoon chopped fresh thyme	Zest and juice of 1 lemon
Sea salt and freshly ground	Flaky sea salt, for serving (optional)

1. In a medium bowl, toss together the asparagus, avocado oil, and thyme, and season with sea salt and pepper. 2. Place the asparagus in the air fryer basket in a single layer. Set the air fryer to 400ºF (204ºC) and air fry for 4 to 8 minutes, to your desired doneness. 3. Transfer to a serving platter. Top with the goat cheese, lemon zest, and lemon juice. If desired, season with a pinch of flaky salt.

Per Serving:
Calories: 121 | fat: 9g | protein: 7g | carbs: 6g | fiber: 3g | sodium: 208mg

Broccoli Salad

Prep time: 5 minutes | Cook time: 7 minutes | Serves 4

2 cups fresh broccoli florets, chopped	pepper
1 tablespoon olive oil	¼ cup lemon juice, divided
¼ teaspoon salt	¼ cup shredded Parmesan cheese
⅛ teaspoon ground black	¼ cup sliced roasted almonds

1. In a large bowl, toss broccoli and olive oil together. Sprinkle with salt and pepper, then drizzle with 2 tablespoons lemon juice. 2. Place broccoli into ungreased air fryer basket. Adjust the temperature to 350ºF (177ºC) and set the timer for 7 minutes, shaking the basket halfway through cooking. Broccoli will be golden on the edges when done. 3. Place broccoli into a large serving bowl and drizzle with remaining lemon juice. Sprinkle with Parmesan and almonds. Serve warm.

Per Serving:
Calories: 76 | fat: 5g | protein: 3g | carbs: 5g | fiber: 1g | sodium: 273mg

Balsamic Brussels Sprouts

Prep time: 5 minutes | Cook time: 12 minutes | Serves 4

2 cups trimmed and halved fresh Brussels sprouts	pepper
2 tablespoons olive oil	2 tablespoons balsamic vinegar
¼ teaspoon salt	2 slices cooked sugar-free bacon, crumbled
¼ teaspoon ground black	

1. In a large bowl, toss Brussels sprouts in olive oil, then sprinkle with salt and pepper. Place into ungreased air fryer basket. Adjust the temperature to 375ºF (191ºC) and set the timer for 12 minutes, shaking the basket halfway through cooking. Brussels sprouts will be tender and browned when done. 2. Place sprouts in a large serving dish and drizzle with balsamic vinegar. Sprinkle bacon over top. Serve warm.

Per Serving:
Calories: 114| fat: 9g | protein: 4g | carbs: 6g | net carbs: 4g | fiber: 2g

Baked Jalapeño and Cheese Cauliflower Mash

Prep time: 10 minutes | Cook time: 15 minutes | Serves 6

1 (12-ounce / 340-g) steamer bag cauliflower florets, cooked according to package instructions	softened
	½ cup shredded sharp Cheddar cheese
	¼ cup pickled jalapeños
2 tablespoons salted butter, softened	½ teaspoon salt
	¼ teaspoon ground black
2 ounces (57 g) cream cheese,	pepper

1. Place cooked cauliflower into a food processor with remaining ingredients. Pulse twenty times until cauliflower is smooth and all ingredients are combined. 2. Spoon mash into an ungreased round nonstick baking dish. Place dish into air fryer basket. Adjust the temperature to 380ºF (193ºC) and bake for 15 minutes. The top will be golden brown when done. Serve warm.

Per Serving:
Calories: 120| fat: 9g | protein: 6g | carbs: 6g | net carbs: 3g | fiber: 3g

Kohlrabi Fries

Prep time: 10 minutes | Cook time: 20 to 30 minutes | Serves 4

2 pounds (907 g) kohlrabi, peeled and cut into ¼ to ½-inch fries	2 tablespoons olive oil
	Salt and freshly ground black pepper, to taste

1. Preheat the air fryer to 400ºF (204ºC). 2. In a large bowl, combine the kohlrabi and olive oil. Season to taste with salt and black pepper. Toss gently until thoroughly coated. 3. Working in batches if necessary, spread the kohlrabi in a single layer in the air fryer basket. Pausing halfway through the cooking time to shake the basket, air fry for 20 to 30 minutes until the fries are lightly browned and crunchy.

Per Serving:
Calories: 121 | fat: 7g | protein: 4g | carbs: 14g | fiber: 8g | sodium: 45mg

Flatbread

Prep time: 5 minutes | Cook time: 7 minutes | Serves 2

1 cup shredded Mozzarella cheese	almond flour
	1 ounce (28 g) full-fat cream
¼ cup blanched finely ground	cheese, softened

1. In a large microwave-safe bowl, melt Mozzarella in the microwave for 30 seconds. Stir in almond flour until smooth and

then add cream cheese. Continue mixing until dough forms, gently kneading it with wet hands if necessary. 2. Divide the dough into two pieces and roll out to ¼-inch thickness between two pieces of parchment. Cut another piece of parchment to fit your air fryer basket. 3. Place a piece of flatbread onto your parchment and into the air fryer, working in two batches if needed. 4. Adjust the temperature to 320ºF (160ºC) and air fry for 7 minutes. 5. Halfway through the cooking time flip the flatbread. Serve warm.

Per Serving:
Calories: 235 | fat: 14g | protein: 23g | carbs: 6g | fiber: 3g | sodium: 475mg

Dijon Roast Cabbage

Prep time: 10 minutes | Cook time: 10 minutes | Serves 4

1 small head cabbage, cored and sliced into 1-inch-thick slices	½ teaspoon salt
	1 tablespoon Dijon mustard
	1 teaspoon apple cider vinegar
2 tablespoons olive oil, divided	1 teaspoon granular erythritol

1. Drizzle each cabbage slice with 1 tablespoon olive oil, then sprinkle with salt. Place slices into ungreased air fryer basket, working in batches if needed. Adjust the temperature to 350ºF (177ºC) and air fry for 10 minutes. Cabbage will be tender and edges will begin to brown when done. 2. In a small bowl, whisk remaining olive oil with mustard, vinegar, and erythritol. Drizzle over cabbage in a large serving dish. Serve warm.

Per Serving:
Calories: 110 | fat: 7.34g | protein: 2.5g | carbs: 10.74g | sugars: 5.47g | fiber: 3.1g | sodium: 392mg

Ratatouille

Prep time: 15 minutes | Cook time: 20 minutes | Serves 2 to 3

2 cups ¾-inch cubed peeled eggplant	halved lengthwise
	3 tablespoons olive oil
1 small red, yellow, or orange bell pepper, stemmed, seeded, and diced	1 teaspoon dried oregano
	½ teaspoon dried thyme
	1 teaspoon kosher salt
1 cup cherry tomatoes	½ teaspoon black pepper
6 to 8 cloves garlic, peeled and	

1. In a medium bowl, combine the eggplant, bell pepper, tomatoes, garlic, oil, oregano, thyme, salt, and pepper. Toss to combine. 2. Place the vegetables in the air fryer basket. Set the air fryer to 400ºF (204ºC) for 20 minutes, or until the vegetables are crisp-tender.

Per Serving:
Calories: 161 | fat: 14g | protein: 2g | carbs: 9g | fiber: 3g | sodium: 781mg

Lemon-Garlic Mushrooms

Prep time: 10 minutes | Cook time: 10 to 15 minutes | Serves 6

12 ounces (340 g) sliced mushrooms
1 tablespoon avocado oil
Sea salt and freshly ground black pepper, to taste
3 tablespoons unsalted butter

1 teaspoon minced garlic
1 teaspoon freshly squeezed lemon juice
½ teaspoon red pepper flakes
2 tablespoons chopped fresh parsley

1. Place the mushrooms in a medium bowl and toss with the oil. Season to taste with salt and pepper. 2. Place the mushrooms in a single layer in the air fryer basket. Set your air fryer to 375°F (191°C) and roast for 10 to 15 minutes, until the mushrooms are tender. 3. While the mushrooms cook, melt the butter in a small pot or skillet over medium-low heat. Stir in the garlic and cook for 30 seconds. Remove the pot from the heat and stir in the lemon juice and red pepper flakes. 4. Toss the mushrooms with the lemon-garlic butter and garnish with the parsley before serving.

Per Serving:

Calories: 72| fat: 6g | protein: 2g | carbs: 3g | net carbs: 2g | fiber: 1g

Radish Chips

Prep time: 10 minutes | Cook time: 5 minutes | Serves 4

2 cups water
1 pound (454 g) radishes
¼ teaspoon onion powder
¼ teaspoon paprika

½ teaspoon garlic powder
2 tablespoons coconut oil, melted

1. Place water in a medium saucepan and bring to a boil on stovetop. 2. Remove the top and bottom from each radish, then use a mandoline to slice each radish thin and uniformly. You may also use the slicing blade in the food processor for this step. 3. Place the radish slices into the boiling water for 5 minutes or until translucent. Remove them from the water and place them into a clean kitchen towel to absorb excess moisture. 4. Toss the radish chips in a large bowl with remaining ingredients until fully coated in oil and seasoning. Place radish chips into the air fryer basket. 5. Adjust the temperature to 320°F (160°C) and air fry for 5 minutes. 6. Shake the basket two or three times during the cooking time. Serve warm.

Per Serving:

Calories: 81 | fat: 7g | protein: 1g | carbs: 5g | fiber: 2g | sodium: 27mg

Curry Roasted Cauliflower

Prep time: 10 minutes | Cook time: 20 minutes | Serves 4

¼ cup olive oil
2 teaspoons curry powder
½ teaspoon salt
¼ teaspoon freshly ground black pepper

1 head cauliflower, cut into bite-size florets
½ red onion, sliced
2 tablespoons freshly chopped parsley, for garnish (optional)

1. Preheat the air fryer to 400°F (204°C). 2. In a large bowl, combine the olive oil, curry powder, salt, and pepper. Add the cauliflower and onion. Toss gently until the vegetables are completely coated with the oil mixture. Transfer the vegetables to the basket of the air fryer. 3. Pausing about halfway through the cooking time to shake the basket, air fry for 20 minutes until the cauliflower is tender and beginning to brown. Top with the parsley, if desired, before serving.

Per Serving:

Calories: 141 | fat: 14g | protein: 2g | carbs: 4g | fiber: 2g | sodium: 312mg

Herbed Shiitake Mushrooms

Prep time: 10 minutes | Cook time: 5 minutes | Serves 4

8 ounces (227 g) shiitake mushrooms, stems removed and caps roughly chopped
1 tablespoon olive oil
½ teaspoon salt
Freshly ground black pepper, to taste

1 teaspoon chopped fresh thyme leaves
1 teaspoon chopped fresh oregano
1 tablespoon chopped fresh parsley

1. Preheat the air fryer to 400°F (204°C). 2. Toss the mushrooms with the olive oil, salt, pepper, thyme and oregano. Air fry for 5 minutes, shaking the basket once or twice during the cooking process. The mushrooms will still be somewhat chewy with a meaty texture. If you'd like them a little more tender, add a couple of minutes to this cooking time. 3. Once cooked, add the parsley to the mushrooms and toss. Season again to taste and serve.

Per Serving:

Calories: 50 | fat: 4g | protein: 1g | carbs: 4g | fiber: 2g | sodium: 296mg

Dinner Rolls

Prep time: 10 minutes | Cook time: 12 minutes | Serves 6

1 cup shredded Mozzarella cheese

1 ounce (28 g) full-fat cream cheese

1 cup blanched finely ground

almond flour

¼ cup ground flaxseed

½ teaspoon baking powder

1 large egg

1. Place Mozzarella, cream cheese, and almond flour in a large microwave-safe bowl. Microwave for 1 minute. Mix until smooth. 2. Add flaxseed, baking powder, and egg until fully combined and smooth. Microwave an additional 15 seconds if it becomes too firm. 3. Separate the dough into six pieces and roll into balls. Place the balls into the air fryer basket. 4. Adjust the temperature to 320ºF (160ºC) and air fry for 12 minutes. 5. Allow rolls to cool completely before serving.

Per Serving:

Calories: 223 | fat: 17g | protein: 13g | carbs: 7g | fiber: 4g | sodium: 175mg

Fried Asparagus

Prep time: 5 minutes | Cook time: 12 minutes | Serves 4

1 tablespoon olive oil

1 pound (454 g) asparagus spears, ends trimmed

¼ teaspoon salt

¼ teaspoon ground black pepper

1 tablespoon salted butter, melted

1. In a large bowl, drizzle olive oil over asparagus spears and sprinkle with salt and pepper. 2. Place spears into ungreased air fryer basket. Adjust the temperature to 375ºF (191ºC) and set the timer for 12 minutes, shaking the basket halfway through cooking. Asparagus will be lightly browned and tender when done. 3. Transfer to a large dish and drizzle with butter. Serve warm.

Per Serving:

Calories: 70| fat: 5g | protein: 3g | carbs: 5g | net carbs: 2g | fiber: 3g

Garlic and Thyme Tomatoes

Prep time: 10 minutes | Cook time: 15 minutes |
Serves 2 to 4

4 Roma tomatoes

1 tablespoon olive oil

Salt and freshly ground black

pepper, to taste

1 clove garlic, minced

½ teaspoon dried thyme

1. Preheat the air fryer to 390ºF (199ºC). 2. Cut the tomatoes in half and scoop out the seeds and any pithy parts with your fingers. Place the tomatoes in a bowl and toss with the olive oil, salt, pepper, garlic and thyme. 3. Transfer the tomatoes to the air fryer, cut side up. Air fry for 15 minutes. The edges should just start to brown. Let the tomatoes cool to an edible temperature for a few minutes and then use in pastas, on top of crostini, or as an accompaniment to any poultry, meat or fish.

Per Serving:

Calories: 56 | fat: 5g | protein: 1g | carbs: 4g | fiber: 1g | sodium: 4mg

Zesty Fried Asparagus

Prep time: 3 minutes | Cook time: 10 minutes | Serves 4

Oil, for spraying

10 to 12 spears asparagus, trimmed

2 tablespoons olive oil

1 tablespoon granulated garlic

1 teaspoon chili powder

½ teaspoon ground cumin

¼ teaspoon salt

1. Line the air fryer basket with parchment and spray lightly with oil. 2. If the asparagus are too long to fit easily in the air fryer, cut them in half. 3. Place the asparagus, olive oil, garlic, chili powder, cumin, and salt in a zip-top plastic bag, seal, and toss until evenly coated. 4. Place the asparagus in the prepared basket. 5. Roast at 390ºF (199ºC) for 5 minutes, flip, and cook for another 5 minutes, or until bright green and firm but tender.

Per Serving:

Calories: 74 | fat: 7g | protein: 1g | carbs: 3g | fiber: 1g | sodium: 166mg

Chapter 7 Vegetarian Mains

Spinach-Artichoke Stuffed Mushrooms

Prep time: 10 minutes | Cook time: 10 to 14 minutes | Serves 4

2 tablespoons olive oil
4 large portobello mushrooms, stems removed and gills scraped out
½ teaspoon salt
¼ teaspoon freshly ground pepper
4 ounces (113 g) goat cheese, crumbled
½ cup chopped marinated artichoke hearts
1 cup frozen spinach, thawed and squeezed dry
½ cup grated Parmesan cheese
2 tablespoons chopped fresh parsley

1. Preheat the air fryer to 400ºF (204ºC). 2. Rub the olive oil over the portobello mushrooms until thoroughly coated. Sprinkle both sides with the salt and black pepper. Place top-side down on a clean work surface. 3. In a small bowl, combine the goat cheese, artichoke hearts, and spinach. Mash with the back of a fork until thoroughly combined. Divide the cheese mixture among the mushrooms and sprinkle with the Parmesan cheese. 4. Air fry for 10 to 14 minutes until the mushrooms are tender and the cheese has begun to brown. Top with the fresh parsley just before serving.
Per Serving:
Calories: 284 | fat: 21g | protein: 16g | carbs: 10g | fiber: 4g | sodium: 686mg

Caprese Eggplant Stacks

Prep time: 5 minutes | Cook time: 12 minutes | Serves 4

1 medium eggplant, cut into ¼-inch slices
2 large tomatoes, cut into ¼-inch slices
4 ounces (113 g) fresh Mozzarella, cut into ½-ounce / 14-g slices
2 tablespoons olive oil
¼ cup fresh basil, sliced

1. In a baking dish, place four slices of eggplant on the bottom. Place a slice of tomato on top of each eggplant round, then Mozzarella, then eggplant. Repeat as necessary. 2. Drizzle with olive oil. Cover dish with foil and place dish into the air fryer basket. 3. Adjust the temperature to 350ºF (177ºC) and bake for 12 minutes. 4. When done, eggplant will be tender. Garnish with fresh basil to serve.
Per Serving:
Calories: 97 | fat: 7g | protein: 2g | carbs: 8g | fiber: 4g | sodium: 11mg

Cheese Stuffed Zucchini

Prep time: 20 minutes | Cook time: 8 minutes | Serves 4

1 large zucchini, cut into four pieces
2 tablespoons olive oil
1 cup Ricotta cheese, room temperature
2 tablespoons scallions, chopped
1 heaping tablespoon fresh parsley, roughly chopped
1 heaping tablespoon coriander, minced
2 ounces (57 g) Cheddar cheese, preferably freshly grated
1 teaspoon celery seeds
½ teaspoon salt
½ teaspoon garlic pepper

1. Cook your zucchini in the air fryer basket for approximately 10 minutes at 350ºF (177ºC). Check for doneness and cook for 2-3 minutes longer if needed. 2. Meanwhile, make the stuffing by mixing the other items. 3. When your zucchini is thoroughly cooked, open them up. Divide the stuffing among all zucchini pieces and bake an additional 5 minutes.
Per Serving:
Calories: 242 | fat: 20g | protein: 12g | carbs: 5g | fiber: 1g | sodium: 443mg

Crispy Cabbage Steaks

Prep time: 5 minutes | Cook time: 10 minutes | Serves 4

1 small head green cabbage, cored and cut into ½-inch-thick slices
¼ teaspoon salt
¼ teaspoon ground black pepper
2 tablespoons olive oil
1 clove garlic, peeled and finely minced
½ teaspoon dried thyme
½ teaspoon dried parsley

1. Sprinkle each side of cabbage with salt and pepper, then place into ungreased air fryer basket, working in batches if needed. 2. Drizzle each side of cabbage with olive oil, then sprinkle with remaining ingredients on both sides. Adjust the temperature to 350ºF (177ºC) and air fry for 10 minutes, turning "steaks" halfway through cooking. 3.Cabbage will be browned at the edges and tender when done. Serve warm.
Per Serving:
Calories: 63 | fat: 7g | protein: 0g | carbs: 1g | fiber: 0g | sodium: 155mg

Vegetable Burgers

Prep time: 10 minutes | Cook time: 12 minutes | Serves 4

8 ounces (227 g) cremini mushrooms
2 large egg yolks
½ medium zucchini, trimmed and chopped
¼ cup peeled and chopped

yellow onion
1 clove garlic, peeled and finely minced
½ teaspoon salt
¼ teaspoon ground black pepper

1. Place all ingredients into a food processor and pulse twenty times until finely chopped and combined. 2. Separate mixture into four equal sections and press each into a burger shape. Place burgers into ungreased air fryer basket. Adjust the temperature to 375°F (191°C) and air fry for 12 minutes, turning burgers halfway through cooking. Burgers will be browned and firm when done. 3. Place burgers on a large plate and let cool 5 minutes before serving.

Per Serving:
Calories: 50 | fat: 3g | protein: 3g | carbs: 4g | fiber: 1g | sodium: 299mg

Roasted Veggie Bowl

Prep time: 10 minutes | Cook time: 15 minutes | Serves 2

1 cup broccoli florets
1 cup quartered Brussels sprouts
½ cup cauliflower florets
¼ medium white onion, peeled and sliced ¼ inch thick

½ medium green bell pepper, seeded and sliced ¼ inch thick
1 tablespoon coconut oil
2 teaspoons chili powder
½ teaspoon garlic powder
½ teaspoon cumin

1. Toss all ingredients together in a large bowl until vegetables are fully coated with oil and seasoning. 2. Pour vegetables into the air fryer basket. 3. Adjust the temperature to 360°F (182°C) and roast for 15 minutes. 4. Shake two or three times during cooking. Serve warm.

Per Serving:
Calories: 112 | fat: 7.68g | protein: 3.64g | carbs: 10.67g | sugars: 3.08g | fiber: 4.6g | sodium: 106mg

Crustless Spinach Cheese Pie

Prep time: 10 minutes | Cook time: 20 minutes | Serves 4

6 large eggs
¼ cup heavy whipping cream
1 cup frozen chopped spinach, drained

1 cup shredded sharp Cheddar cheese
¼ cup diced yellow onion

1. In a medium bowl, whisk eggs and add cream. Add remaining ingredients to bowl. 2. Pour into a round baking dish. Place into the air fryer basket. 3. Adjust the temperature to 320°F (160°C)

and bake for 20 minutes. 4. Eggs will be firm and slightly browned when cooked. Serve immediately.

Per Serving:
Calories: 263 | fat: 20g | protein: 18g | carbs: 4g | fiber: 1g | sodium: 321mg

Three-Cheese Zucchini Boats

Prep time: 15 minutes | Cook time: 20 minutes | Serves 2

2 medium zucchini
1 tablespoon avocado oil
¼ cup low-carb, no-sugar-added pasta sauce
¼ cup full-fat ricotta cheese
¼ cup shredded Mozzarella

cheese
¼ teaspoon dried oregano
¼ teaspoon garlic powder
½ teaspoon dried parsley
2 tablespoons grated vegetarian Parmesan cheese

1. Cut off 1 inch from the top and bottom of each zucchini. Slice zucchini in half lengthwise and use a spoon to scoop out a bit of the inside, making room for filling. Brush with oil and spoon 2 tablespoons pasta sauce into each shell. 2. In a medium bowl, mix ricotta, Mozzarella, oregano, garlic powder, and parsley. Spoon the mixture into each zucchini shell. Place stuffed zucchini shells into the air fryer basket. 3. Adjust the temperature to 350°F (177°C) and air fry for 20 minutes. 4. To remove from the basket, use tongs or a spatula and carefully lift out. Top with Parmesan. Serve immediately.

Per Serving:
Calories: 208 | fat: 14g | protein: 12g | carbs: 11g | fiber: 3g | sodium: 247mg

Cheesy Cauliflower Pizza Crust

Prep time: 15 minutes | Cook time: 11 minutes | Serves 2

1 (12-ounce / 340-g) steamer bag cauliflower
½ cup shredded sharp Cheddar cheese
1 large egg

2 tablespoons blanched finely ground almond flour
1 teaspoon Italian blend seasoning

1. Cook cauliflower according to package instructions. Remove from bag and place into cheesecloth or paper towel to remove excess water. Place cauliflower into a large bowl. 2. Add cheese, egg, almond flour, and Italian seasoning to the bowl and mix well. 3. Cut a piece of parchment to fit your air fryer basket. Press cauliflower into 6-inch round circle. Place into the air fryer basket. 4. Adjust the temperature to 360°F (182°C) and air fry for 11 minutes. 5. After 7 minutes, flip the pizza crust. 6. Add preferred toppings to pizza. Place back into air fryer basket and cook an additional 4 minutes or until fully cooked and golden. Serve immediately.

Per Serving:
Calories: 251 | fat: 17g | protein: 15g | carbs: 12g | fiber: 5g | sodium: 375mg

Cauliflower Steak with Gremolata

Prep time: 15 minutes | Cook time: 25 minutes | Serves 4

2 tablespoons olive oil
1 tablespoon Italian seasoning
1 large head cauliflower, outer leaves removed and sliced lengthwise through the core into thick "steaks"
Salt and freshly ground black pepper, to taste
¼ cup Parmesan cheese

Gremolata:
1 bunch Italian parsley (about 1 cup packed)
2 cloves garlic
Zest of 1 small lemon, plus 1 to 2 teaspoons lemon juice
½ cup olive oil
Salt and pepper, to taste

1. Preheat the air fryer to 400°F (204°C). 2. In a small bowl, combine the olive oil and Italian seasoning. Brush both sides of each cauliflower "steak" generously with the oil. Season to taste with salt and black pepper. 3. Working in batches if necessary, arrange the cauliflower in a single layer in the air fryer basket. Pausing halfway through the cooking time to turn the "steaks," air fry for 15 to 20 minutes until the cauliflower is tender and the edges begin to brown. Sprinkle with the Parmesan and air fry for 5 minutes longer. 4. To make the gremolata: In a food processor fitted with a metal blade, combine the parsley, garlic, and lemon zest and juice. With the motor running, add the olive oil in a steady stream until the mixture forms a bright green sauce. Season to taste with salt and black pepper. Serve the cauliflower steaks with the gremolata spooned over the top.

Per Serving:
Calories: 336 | fat: 30g | protein: 7g | carbs: 15g | fiber: 5g | sodium: 340mg

Mediterranean Pan Pizza

Prep time: 5 minutes | Cook time: 8 minutes | Serves 2

1 cup shredded Mozzarella cheese
¼ medium red bell pepper, seeded and chopped
½ cup chopped fresh spinach leaves
2 tablespoons chopped black olives
2 tablespoons crumbled feta cheese

1. Sprinkle Mozzarella into an ungreased round nonstick baking dish in an even layer. Add remaining ingredients on top. 2. Place dish into air fryer basket. Adjust the temperature to 350°F (177°C) and bake for 8 minutes, checking halfway through to avoid burning. Top of pizza will be golden brown and the cheese melted when done. 3. Remove dish from fryer and let cool 5 minutes before slicing and serving.

Per Serving:
Calories: 108 | fat: 1g | protein: 20g | carbs: 5g | fiber: 3g | sodium: 521mg

Broccoli-Cheese Fritters

Prep time: 5 minutes | Cook time: 20 to 25 minutes | Serves 4

1 cup broccoli florets
1 cup shredded Mozzarella cheese
¾ cup almond flour
½ cup flaxseed meal, divided
2 teaspoons baking powder

1 teaspoon garlic powder
Salt and freshly ground black pepper, to taste
2 eggs, lightly beaten
½ cup ranch dressing

1. Preheat the air fryer to 400°F (204°C). 2. In a food processor fitted with a metal blade, pulse the broccoli until very finely chopped. 3. Transfer the broccoli to a large bowl and add the Mozzarella, almond flour, ¼ cup of the flaxseed meal, baking powder, and garlic powder. Stir until thoroughly combined. Season to taste with salt and black pepper. Add the eggs and stir again to form a sticky dough. Shape the dough into 1¼-inch fritters. 4. Place the remaining ¼ cup flaxseed meal in a shallow bowl and roll the fritters in the meal to form an even coating. 5. Working in batches if necessary, arrange the fritters in a single layer in the basket of the air fryer and spray generously with olive oil. Pausing halfway through the cooking time to shake the basket, air fry for 20 to 25 minutes until the fritters are golden brown and crispy. Serve with the ranch dressing for dipping.

Per Serving:
Calories: 388 | fat: 30g | protein: 19g | carbs: 14g | fiber: 7g | sodium: 526mg

Stuffed Portobellos

Prep time: 10 minutes | Cook time: 8 minutes | Serves 4

3 ounces (85 g) cream cheese, softened
½ medium zucchini, trimmed and chopped
¼ cup seeded and chopped red bell pepper
1½ cups chopped fresh spinach

leaves
4 large portobello mushrooms, stems removed
2 tablespoons coconut oil, melted
½ teaspoon salt

1. In a medium bowl, mix cream cheese, zucchini, pepper, and spinach. 2. Drizzle mushrooms with coconut oil and sprinkle with salt. Scoop ¼ zucchini mixture into each mushroom. 3. Place mushrooms into ungreased air fryer basket. Adjust the temperature to 400°F (204°C) and air fry for 8 minutes. Portobellos will be tender and tops will be browned when done. Serve warm.

Per Serving:
Calories: 151 | fat: 13g | protein: 4g | carbs: 6g | fiber: 2g | sodium: 427mg

Pesto Vegetable Skewers

Prep time: 30 minutes | Cook time: 8 minutes | Makes 8 skewers

1 medium zucchini, trimmed and cut into ½-inch slices	squares
	16 whole cremini mushrooms
½ medium yellow onion, peeled and cut into 1-inch squares	⅓ cup basil pesto
	½ teaspoon salt
1 medium red bell pepper, seeded and cut into 1-inch	¼ teaspoon ground black pepper

1. Divide zucchini slices, onion, and bell pepper into eight even portions. Place on 6-inch skewers for a total of eight kebabs. Add 2 mushrooms to each skewer and brush kebabs generously with pesto. 2. Sprinkle each kebab with salt and black pepper on all sides, then place into ungreased air fryer basket. Adjust the temperature to 375ºF (191ºC) and air fry for 8 minutes, turning kebabs halfway through cooking. Vegetables will be browned at the edges and tender-crisp when done. Serve warm.

Per Serving:
Calories: 75 | fat: 6g | protein: 3g | carbs: 4g | fiber: 1g | sodium: 243mg

Eggplant Parmesan

Prep time: 15 minutes | Cook time: 17 minutes | Serves 4

1 medium eggplant, ends trimmed, sliced into ½-inch rounds	1 ounce (28 g) 100% cheese crisps, finely crushed
¼ teaspoon salt	½ cup low-carb marinara sauce
2 tablespoons coconut oil	½ cup shredded Mozzarella cheese
½ cup grated Parmesan cheese	

1. Sprinkle eggplant rounds with salt on both sides and wrap in a kitchen towel for 30 minutes. Press to remove excess water, then drizzle rounds with coconut oil on both sides. 2. In a medium bowl, mix Parmesan and cheese crisps. Press each eggplant slice into mixture to coat both sides. 3. Place rounds into ungreased air fryer basket. Adjust the temperature to 350ºF (177ºC) and air fry for 15 minutes, turning rounds halfway through cooking. They will be crispy around the edges when done. 4. Spoon marinara over rounds and sprinkle with Mozzarella. Continue cooking an additional 2 minutes at 350ºF (177ºC) until cheese is melted. Serve warm.

Per Serving:
Calories: 208 | fat: 13g | protein: 12g | carbs: 13g | fiber: 5g | sodium: 531mg

Cauliflower Rice-Stuffed Peppers

Prep time: 10 minutes | Cook time: 15 minutes | Serves 4

2 cups uncooked cauliflower rice	cheese
	¼ teaspoon salt
¾ cup drained canned petite diced tomatoes	¼ teaspoon ground black pepper
2 tablespoons olive oil	4 medium green bell peppers,
1 cup shredded Mozzarella	tops removed, seeded

1. In a large bowl, mix all ingredients except bell peppers. Scoop mixture evenly into peppers. 2. Place peppers into ungreased air fryer basket. Adjust the temperature to 350ºF (177ºC) and air fry for 15 minutes. Peppers will be tender and cheese will be melted when done. Serve warm.

Per Serving:
Calories: 144 | fat: 7g | protein: 11g | carbs: 11g | fiber: 5g | sodium: 380mg

Pesto Spinach Flatbread

Prep time: 10 minutes | Cook time: 8 minutes | Serves 4

1 cup blanched finely ground almond flour	cheese
	1 cup chopped fresh spinach leaves
2 ounces (57 g) cream cheese	
2 cups shredded Mozzarella	2 tablespoons basil pesto

1. Place flour, cream cheese, and Mozzarella in a large microwave-safe bowl and microwave on high 45 seconds, then stir. 2. Fold in spinach and microwave an additional 15 seconds. Stir until a soft dough ball forms. 3. Cut two pieces of parchment paper to fit air fryer basket. Separate dough into two sections and press each out on ungreased parchment to create 6-inch rounds. 4. Spread 1 tablespoon pesto over each flatbread and place rounds on parchment into ungreased air fryer basket. Adjust the temperature to 350ºF (177ºC) and air fry for 8 minutes, turning crusts halfway through cooking. Flatbread will be golden when done. 5. Let cool 5 minutes before slicing and serving.

Per Serving:
Calories: 387 | fat: 28g | protein: 28g | carbs: 10g | fiber: 5g | sodium: 556mg

Chapter 8 Desserts

Double Chocolate Brownies

Prep time: 5 minutes | Cook time: 15 to 20 minutes | Serves 8

1 cup almond flour	½ cup unsalted butter, melted
½ cup unsweetened cocoa powder	and cooled
	3 eggs
½ teaspoon baking powder	1 teaspoon vanilla extract
⅓ cup Swerve	2 tablespoons mini semisweet
¼ teaspoon salt	chocolate chips

1. Preheat the air fryer to 350°F (177°C). Line a cake pan with parchment paper and brush with oil. 2. In a large bowl, combine the almond flour, cocoa powder, baking powder, Swerve, and salt. Add the butter, eggs, and vanilla. Stir until thoroughly combined. (The batter will be thick.) Spread the batter into the prepared pan and scatter the chocolate chips on top. 3. Air fry for 15 to 20 minutes until the edges are set. (The center should still appear slightly undercooked.) Let cool completely before slicing. To store, cover and refrigerate the brownies for up to 3 days.

Per Serving:

Calories: 191 | fat: 17g | protein: 6g | carbs: 7g | net carbs: 3g | fiber: 4g

Pumpkin Cookie with Cream Cheese Frosting

Prep time: 10 minutes | Cook time: 7 minutes | Serves 6

½ cup blanched finely ground almond flour	½ teaspoon pumpkin pie spice
	2 tablespoons pure pumpkin
½ cup powdered erythritol, divided	purée
	½ teaspoon ground cinnamon,
2 tablespoons butter, softened	divided
1 large egg	¼ cup low-carb, sugar-free
½ teaspoon unflavored gelatin	chocolate chips
½ teaspoon baking powder	3 ounces (85 g) full-fat cream
½ teaspoon vanilla extract	cheese, softened

1. In a large bowl, mix almond flour and ¼ cup erythritol. Stir in butter, egg, and gelatin until combined. 2. Stir in baking powder, vanilla, pumpkin pie spice, pumpkin purée, and ¼ teaspoon cinnamon, then fold in chocolate chips. 3. Pour batter into a round baking pan. Place pan into the air fryer basket. 4. Adjust the temperature to 300°F (149°C) and bake for 7 minutes. 5. When fully cooked, the top will be golden brown and a toothpick inserted in center will come out clean. Let cool at least 20 minutes. 6. To make the frosting: mix cream cheese, remaining ¼ teaspoon cinnamon, and remaining ¼ cup erythritol in a large bowl. Using an electric mixer, beat until it becomes fluffy. Spread onto the cooled cookie. Garnish with additional cinnamon if desired.

Per Serving:

Calories: 186 | fat: 16g | protein: 4g | carbs: 5g | net carbs: 4g | fiber: 2g

Chocolate Lava Cakes

Prep time: 5 minutes | Cook time: 15 minutes | Serves 2

2 large eggs, whisked	½ teaspoon vanilla extract
¼ cup blanched finely ground almond flour	2 ounces (57 g) low-carb chocolate chips, melted

1. In a medium bowl, mix eggs with flour and vanilla. Fold in chocolate until fully combined. 2. Pour batter into two ramekins greased with cooking spray. Place ramekins into air fryer basket. Adjust the temperature to 320°F (160°C) and bake for 15 minutes. Cakes will be set at the edges and firm in the center when done. Let cool 5 minutes before serving.

Per Serving:

Calories: 313 | fat: 23g | protein: 11g | carbs: 16g | fiber: 5g | sodium: 77mg

Vanilla Scones

Prep time: 20 minutes | Cook time: 10 minutes | Serves 6

4 ounces (113 g) coconut flour	¼ cup heavy cream
½ teaspoon baking powder	1 teaspoon vanilla extract
1 teaspoon apple cider vinegar	1 tablespoon erythritol
2 teaspoons mascarpone	Cooking spray

1. In the mixing bowl, mix coconut flour with baking powder, apple cider vinegar, mascarpone, heavy cream, vanilla extract, and erythritol. 2. Knead the dough and cut into scones. 3. Then put them in the air fryer basket and sprinkle with cooking spray. 4. Cook the vanilla scones at 365°F (185°C) for 10 minutes.

Per Serving:

Calories: 87 | fat: 8g | protein: 1g | carbs: 3g | net carbs: 1g | fiber: 2g

Halle Berries-and-Cream Cobbler

Prep time: 10 minutes | Cook time: 25 minutes | Serves 4

12 ounces (340 g) cream cheese (1½ cups), softened
1 large egg
¾ cup Swerve confectioners'-style sweetener or equivalent amount of powdered sweetener
½ teaspoon vanilla extract
¼ teaspoon fine sea salt
1 cup sliced fresh raspberries or strawberries
Biscuits:
3 large egg whites
¾ cup blanched almond flour
1 teaspoon baking powder
2½ tablespoons very cold

unsalted butter, cut into pieces
¼ teaspoon fine sea salt
Frosting:
2 ounces (57 g) cream cheese (¼ cup), softened
1 tablespoon Swerve confectioners'-style sweetener or equivalent amount of powdered or liquid sweetener
1 tablespoon unsweetened, unflavored almond milk or heavy cream
Fresh raspberries or strawberries, for garnish

1. Preheat the air fryer to 400°F (204°C). Grease a pie pan. 2. In a large mixing bowl, use a hand mixer to combine the cream cheese, egg, and sweetener until smooth. Stir in the vanilla and salt. Gently fold in the raspberries with a rubber spatula. Pour the mixture into the prepared pan and set aside. 3. Make the biscuits: Place the egg whites in a medium-sized mixing bowl or the bowl of a stand mixer. Using a hand mixer or stand mixer, whip the egg whites until very fluffy and stiff. 4. In a separate medium-sized bowl, combine the almond flour and baking powder. Cut in the butter and add the salt, stirring gently to keep the butter pieces intact. 5. Gently fold the almond flour mixture into the egg whites. Use a large spoon or ice cream scooper to scoop out the dough and form it into a 2-inch-wide biscuit, making sure the butter stays in separate clumps. Place the biscuit on top of the raspberry mixture in the pan. Repeat with remaining dough to make 4 biscuits. 6. Place the pan in the air fryer and bake for 5 minutes, then lower the temperature to 325°F (163°C) and bake for another 17 to 20 minutes, until the biscuits are golden brown. 7. While the cobbler cooks, make the frosting: Place the cream cheese in a small bowl and stir to break it up. Add the sweetener and stir. Add the almond milk and stir until well combined. If you prefer a thinner frosting, add more almond milk. 8. Remove the cobbler from the air fryer and allow to cool slightly, then drizzle with the frosting. Garnish with fresh raspberries. 9. Store leftovers in an airtight container in the refrigerator for up to 3 days. Reheat the cobbler in a preheated 350°F (177°C) air fryer for 3 minutes, or until warmed through.

Per Serving:
Calories: 535 | fat: 14g | protein: 13g | carbs: 14g | net carbs: 10g | fiber: 4g

Pretzels

Prep time: 10 minutes | Cook time: 10 minutes | Serves 6

1½ cups shredded Mozzarella cheese
1 cup blanched finely ground almond flour
2 tablespoons salted butter,

melted, divided
¼ cup granular erythritol, divided
1 teaspoon ground cinnamon

1. Place Mozzarella, flour, 1 tablespoon butter, and 2 tablespoons erythritol in a large microwave-safe bowl. Microwave on high 45 seconds, then stir with a fork until a smooth dough ball forms. 2. Separate dough into six equal sections. Gently roll each section into a 12-inch rope, then fold into a pretzel shape. 3. Place pretzels into ungreased air fryer basket. Adjust the temperature to 370°F (188°C) and set the timer for 8 minutes, turning pretzels halfway through cooking. 4. In a small bowl, combine remaining butter, remaining erythritol, and cinnamon. Brush ½ mixture on both sides of pretzels. 5. Place pretzels back into air fryer and cook an additional 2 minutes at 370°F (188°C). 6. Transfer pretzels to a large plate. Brush on both sides with remaining butter mixture, then let cool 5 minutes before serving.

Per Serving:
Calories: 131 | fat: 8g | protein: 11g | carbs: 4g | net carbs: 2g | fiber: 2g

Protein Powder Doughnut Holes

Prep time: 25 minutes | Cook time: 6 minutes | Makes 12 holes

½ cup blanched finely ground almond flour
½ cup low-carb vanilla protein powder
½ cup granular erythritol

½ teaspoon baking powder
1 large egg
5 tablespoons unsalted butter, melted
½ teaspoon vanilla extract

1. Mix all ingredients in a large bowl. Place into the freezer for 20 minutes. 2. Wet your hands with water and roll the dough into twelve balls. 3. Cut a piece of parchment to fit your air fryer basket. Working in batches as necessary, place doughnut holes into the air fryer basket on top of parchment. 4. Adjust the temperature to 380°F (193°C) and air fry for 6 minutes. 5. Flip doughnut holes halfway through the cooking time. 6. Let cool completely before serving.

Per Serving:
1 hole: calories: 89 | fat: 7g | protein: 5g | carbs: 2g | net carbs: 1g | fiber: 1g

New York Cheesecake

Prep time: 1 hour | Cook time: 37 minutes | Serves 8

1½ cups almond flour	½ cup heavy cream
3 ounces (85 g) Swerve	1¼ cups granulated Swerve
½ stick butter, melted	3 eggs, at room temperature
20 ounces (567 g) full-fat cream cheese	1 tablespoon vanilla essence
	1 teaspoon grated lemon zest

1. Coat the sides and bottom of a baking pan with a little flour. 2. In a mixing bowl, combine the almond flour and Swerve. Add the melted butter and mix until your mixture looks like bread crumbs. 3. Press the mixture into the bottom of the prepared pan to form an even layer. Bake at 330°F (166°C) for 7 minutes until golden brown. Allow it to cool completely on a wire rack. 4. Meanwhile, in a mixer fitted with the paddle attachment, prepare the filling by mixing the soft cheese, heavy cream, and granulated Swerve; beat until creamy and fluffy. 5. Crack the eggs into the mixing bowl, one at a time; add the vanilla and lemon zest and continue to mix until fully combined. 6. Pour the prepared topping over the cooled crust and spread evenly. 7. Bake in the preheated air fryer at 330°F (166°C) for 25 to 30 minutes; leave it in the air fryer to keep warm for another 30 minutes. 8. Cover your cheesecake with plastic wrap. Place in your refrigerator and allow it to cool at least 6 hours or overnight. Serve well chilled.

Per Serving:
Calories: 409 | fat: 38g | protein: 10g | carbs: 7g | net carbs: 5g | fiber: 2g

Zucchini Bread

Prep time: 10 minutes | Cook time: 40 minutes | Serves 12

2 cups coconut flour	1 teaspoon vanilla extract
2 teaspoons baking powder	3 eggs, beaten
¾ cup erythritol	1 zucchini, grated
½ cup coconut oil, melted	1 teaspoon ground cinnamon
1 teaspoon apple cider vinegar	

1. In the mixing bowl, mix coconut flour with baking powder, erythritol, coconut oil, apple cider vinegar, vanilla extract, eggs, zucchini, and ground cinnamon. 2. Transfer the mixture into the air fryer basket and flatten it in the shape of the bread. 3. Cook the bread at 350°F (177°C) for 40 minutes.

Per Serving:
Calories: 135 | fat: 14g | protein: 2g | carbs: 4g | net carbs: 3g | fiber: 1g

Crustless Peanut Butter Cheesecake

Prep time: 10 minutes | Cook time: 10 minutes | Serves 2

4 ounces (113 g) cream cheese, softened	1 tablespoon all-natural, no-sugar-added peanut butter
2 tablespoons confectioners' erythritol	½ teaspoon vanilla extract
	1 large egg, whisked

1. In a medium bowl, mix cream cheese and erythritol until smooth. Add peanut butter and vanilla, mixing until smooth. Add egg and stir just until combined. 2. Spoon mixture into an ungreased springform pan and place into air fryer basket. Adjust the temperature to 300°F (149°C) and bake for 10 minutes. Edges will be firm, but center will be mostly set with only a small amount of jiggle when done. 3. Let pan cool at room temperature 30 minutes, cover with plastic wrap, then place into refrigerator at least 2 hours. Serve chilled.

Per Serving:
Calories: 281 | fat: 26g | protein: 8g | carbs: 4g | net carbs: 4g | fiber: 0g

Lime Bars

Prep time: 10 minutes | Cook time: 33 minutes | Makes 12 bars

1½ cups blanched finely ground almond flour, divided	4 tablespoons salted butter, melted
¾ cup confectioners' erythritol, divided	½ cup fresh lime juice
	2 large eggs, whisked

1. In a medium bowl, mix together 1 cup flour, ¼ cup erythritol, and butter. Press mixture into bottom of an ungreased round nonstick cake pan. 2. Place pan into air fryer basket. Adjust the temperature to 300°F (149°C) and bake for 13 minutes. Crust will be brown and set in the middle when done. 3. Allow to cool in pan 10 minutes. 4. In a medium bowl, combine remaining flour, remaining erythritol, lime juice, and eggs. Pour mixture over cooled crust and return to air fryer for 20 minutes at 300°F (149°C). Top will be browned and firm when done. 5. Let cool completely in pan, about 30 minutes, then chill covered in the refrigerator 1 hour. Serve chilled.

Per Serving:
Calories: 144 | fat: 13g | protein: 5g | carbs: 4g | net carbs: 2g | fiber: 2g

Appendix 1 Measurement Conversion Chart

MEASUREMENT CONVERSION CHART

VOLUME EQUIVALENTS(DRY)

US STANDARD	METRIC (APPROXIMATE)
1/8 teaspoon	0.5 mL
1/4 teaspoon	1 mL
1/2 teaspoon	2 mL
3/4 teaspoon	4 mL
1 teaspoon	5 mL
1 tablespoon	15 mL
1/4 cup	59 mL
1/2 cup	118 mL
3/4 cup	177 mL
1 cup	235 mL
2 cups	475 mL
3 cups	700 mL
4 cups	1 L

VOLUME EQUIVALENTS(LIQUID)

US STANDARD	US STANDARD (OUNCES)	METRIC (APPROXIMATE)
2 tablespoons	1 fl.oz.	30 mL
1/4 cup	2 fl.oz.	60 mL
1/2 cup	4 fl.oz.	120 mL
1 cup	8 fl.oz.	240 mL
1 1/2 cup	12 fl.oz.	355 mL
2 cups or 1 pint	16 fl.oz.	475 mL
4 cups or 1 quart	32 fl.oz.	1 L
1 gallon	128 fl.oz.	4 L

TEMPERATURES EQUIVALENTS

FAHRENHEIT(F)	CELSIUS(C) (APPROXIMATE)
225 °F	107 °C
250 °F	120 °C
275 °F	135 °C
300 °F	150 °C
325 °F	160 °C
350 °F	180 °C
375 °F	190 °C
400 °F	205 °C
425 °F	220 °C
450 °F	235 °C
475 °F	245 °C
500 °F	260 °C

WEIGHT EQUIVALENTS

US STANDARD	METRIC (APPROXIMATE)
1 ounce	28 g
2 ounces	57 g
5 ounces	142 g
10 ounces	284 g
15 ounces	425 g
16 ounces (1 pound)	455 g
1.5 pounds	680 g
2 pounds	907 g

Appendix 2 Air Fryer Cooking Chart

Air Fryer Cooking Chart

Beef

Item	Temp (°F)	Time (mins)	Item	Temp (°F)	Time (mins)
Beef Eye Round Roast (4 lbs.)	400 °F	45 to 55	Meatballs (1-inch)	370 °F	7
Burger Patty (4 oz.)	370 °F	16 to 20	Meatballs (3-inch)	380 °F	10
Filet Mignon (8 oz.)	400 °F	18	Ribeye, bone-in (1-inch, 8 oz)	400 °F	10 to 15
Flank Steak (1.5 lbs.)	400 °F	12	Sirloin steaks (1-inch, 12 oz)	400 °F	9 to 14
Flank Steak (2 lbs.)	400 °F	20 to 28			

Chicken

Item	Temp (°F)	Time (mins)	Item	Temp (°F)	Time (mins)
Breasts, bone in (1 ¼ lb.)	370 °F	25	Legs, bone-in (1 ¾ lb.)	380 °F	30
Breasts, boneless (4 oz)	380 °F	12	Thighs, boneless (1 ½ lb.)	380 °F	18 to 20
Drumsticks (2 ½ lb.)	370 °F	20	Wings (2 lb.)	400 °F	12
Game Hen (halved 2 lb.)	390 °F	20	Whole Chicken	360 °F	75
Thighs, bone-in (2 lb.)	380 °F	22	Tenders	360 °F	8 to 10

Pork & Lamb

Item	Temp (°F)	Time (mins)	Item	Temp (°F)	Time (mins)
Bacon (regular)	400 °F	5 to 7	Pork Tenderloin	370 °F	15
Bacon (thick cut)	400 °F	6 to 10	Sausages	380 °F	15
Pork Loin (2 lb.)	360 °F	55	Lamb Loin Chops (1-inch thick)	400 °F	8 to 12
Pork Chops, bone in (1-inch, 6.5 oz)	400 °F	12	Rack of Lamb (1.5 – 2 lb.)	380 °F	22

Fish & Seafood

Item	Temp (°F)	Time (mins)	Item	Temp (°F)	Time (mins)
Calamari (8 oz)	400 °F	4	Tuna Steak	400 °F	7 to 10
Fish Fillet (1-inch, 8 oz)	400 °F	10	Scallops	400 °F	5 to 7
Salmon, fillet (6 oz)	380 °F	12	Shrimp	400 °F	5
Swordfish steak	400 °F	10			

Air Fryer Cooking Chart

		Vegetables			
INGREDIENT	AMOUNT	PREPARATION	OIL	TEMP	COOK TIME
Asparagus	2 bunches	Cut in half, trim stems	2 Tbsp	420°F	12-15 mins
Beets	1½ lbs	Peel, cut in ½-inch cubes	1Tbsp	390°F	28-30 mins
Bell peppers (for roasting)	4 peppers	Cut in quarters, remove seeds	1Tbsp	400°F	15-20 mins
Broccoli	1 large head	Cut in 1-2-inch florets	1Tbsp	400°F	15-20 mins
Brussels sprouts	1lb	Cut in half, remove stems	1Tbsp	425°F	15-20 mins
Carrots	1lb	Peel, cut in ¼-inch rounds	1 Tbsp	425°F	10-15 mins
Cauliflower	1 head	Cut in 1-2-inch florets	2 Tbsp	400°F	20-22 mins
Corn on the cob	7 ears	Whole ears, remove husks	1 Tbps	400°F	14-17 mins
Green beans	1 bag (12 oz)	Trim	1 Tbps	420°F	18-20 mins
Kale (for chips)	4 oz	Tear into pieces,remove stems	None	325°F	5-8 mins
Mushrooms	16 oz	Rinse, slice thinly	1 Tbps	390°F	25-30 mins
Potatoes, russet	1½ lbs	Cut in 1-inch wedges	1 Tbps	390°F	25-30 mins
Potatoes, russet	1lb	Hand-cut fries, soak 30 mins in cold water, then pat dry	½ -3 Tbps	400°F	25-28 mins
Potatoes, sweet	1lb	Hand-cut fries, soak 30 mins in cold water, then pat dry	1 Tbps	400°F	25-28 mins
Zucchini	1lb	Cut in eighths lengthwise, then cut in half	1 Tbps	400°F	15-20 mins

Made in the USA
Monee, IL
13 February 2023

27696464R00042